WITH EAGER HANDS

Elizabeth Coleman White

WITH EAGER HANDS

The Life of Elizabeth Coleman White

By
ALBERTINE SENSKE

South Jersey Culture & History Center

2020

Published in 2020 by the South Jersey Culture & History
Center

South Jersey Culture & History Center, Stockton University,
101 Vera King Farris Drive, Galloway, New Jersey, 08205

Title: With Eager Hands • The Life of Elizabeth Coleman
White

Author: Albertine Senske

ISBN-13: 978-1-947889-02-6

*The South Jersey Culture & History Center is grateful to the Whitesbog
Preservation Trust and its members, past and present, for their invaluable assistance in making the completion of this biography possible.*

Contents

Elizabeth C. White: A Life Well Lived

Photographs

Introduction

Elizabeth Coleman White—horticulturist, conservationist, and social advocate—was an extraordinary woman and one of New Jersey's shining stars, important enough to have been nominated to the state's Hall of Fame. It is serendipitous that New Jersey can claim her and her accomplishments, especially her role in the development of the cultivated blueberry. If all had gone as her father had planned, Elizabeth might have been Wisconsin's boast. Or perhaps she would have lived a quiet, simple life, and been known only to her family and friends. Elizabeth's brother-in-law, Frank Chambers, recounted the following details of her early family life.[1]

After publishing *Cranberry Culture* in 1870, J. J. White, Elizabeth's father, received frequent requests to evaluate land for potential use as cranberry bogs. On a trip to Wisconsin, White liked what he saw and made an investment with two other gentlemen. He secured a home and began to make plans to manage the farm and to relocate his family, but before any of these things materialized, the Wisconsin home he had selected sustained a fire. There was considerable delay in his attempt to replace the house. That, and issues in New Jersey that demanded immediate attention, caused J. J. White to return home. Once there, he stayed, eventually selling his shares in the Grand Marsh, Wisconsin, venture. So it came to be that it was here in the New Jersey Pinelands that Elizabeth learned the life lessons that culminated in a legacy of realized potential, leadership, and courage.

The decision to settle in New Jersey was not the final influence J. J. White had on his daughter's path in life. During a talk delivered to the Wisconsin cranberry growers in 1927, Elizabeth confirmed that initially, at least, she became part of the farming community at J. J.'s wish.

> As a girl, I had various schemes to what I thought I would like to do, and my father pinched them in the bud . . . All my life, I had followed my father's plans and directions in developing cranberry culture.[2]

It is intriguing to speculate about what dreams Elizabeth held in her heart. As we go through Elizabeth's life, it becomes apparent that she had myriad and varied interests. An examination of her written words and the transcripts of her speeches clearly show her abilities as an author. At Whitesbog, she designed the superintendent's house and assisted in the design of her own home,[3] which she called Suningive.[4] An architect perhaps? Her talent for photography presented another career choice. And do not forget her deep interest in matters of social justice. It is not hard to imagine Elizabeth White as a full-time advocate. Were these her aspirations and were there others yet unimagined? They can't be known. It may be that in following her father's plans, Miss White achieved all the above.

Until 1911, Elizabeth C. White lived a relatively sheltered life. It is true that cranberry growers across the United States knew and respected her. Friends and neighbors recognized the care and concern she showed for them and for the workers on the bogs. She often traveled with family not only to nearby locales like Philadelphia, but also to more exotic destinations like Egypt. Yet, in all these interactions, Elizabeth remained a private person. November 1910 would prove to be a turning point in this regard. Elizabeth Coleman White would become known to the world at large. The catalyst for this change was the printed word.

Two works catapulted her into the public sphere. The first was a notice in the November 1910 U. S. Department of Agriculture's list of publications for a pamphlet by Frederick V. Coville on blueberry cultivation. The second was a National Child Labor Committee (NCLC) leaflet that described the perceived injustices that cranberry growers perpetrated on the children of the nation's immigrant working class.

This biography of Elizabeth C. White is arranged in topical, rather than chronological order to present her multifaceted activities and talents better. The early years are relatively easy to follow, being more linear in nature, but from 1911 onward, when Elizabeth begins demonstrating her deft skills as a multitasker, related story threads are examined together. Her father's ill health around this pivotal year may have provided the initial impetus for Elizabeth's added involvements, but once started, she never looked back.

A quick overview of 1911 will exemplify her busy schedule.

- In January 1911, the members of Growers Cranberry Company, the selling arm for most New Jersey and New England cranberry growers, vote to join with the Midwestern growers to form a national cooperative. J. J. White falls ill and delegates to Elizabeth the continuing work of hammering out the details.

- Elizabeth writes to the USDA and receives permission to begin involvement in blueberry cultivation with Frederick Coville.

- J. J. White, who formulated the initial response to accusations made by the National Child Labor Committee against the New Jersey cranberry growers, passes the torch to Elizabeth.

Any one of these endeavors would have presented a daunting challenge. Elizabeth White took them on simultaneously and *with eager hands.*

The selection of a title for this biography was inspired by an article in *Cranberries* magazine. Neil Stevens wrote:

> Somewhere in his "Collected Legal Papers," the late Justice Holmes says: "With all humility I think 'Whatever thy hand findeth to do, do it with thy might' is infinitely more important than the vain attempt to love one's neighbor as oneself." Without attempting to argue the Justice's thesis, I wish merely to say that the quotation reminded me immediately of Elizabeth White.[5]

So, dear reader, I invite you to begin your perusal of these pages. By doing so you will learn to know, respect, admire, and enjoy one of New Jersey's most fascinating women: Elizabeth Coleman White.

Acknowledgments

I am deeply grateful to so many people for their help on the long road to getting this book written and published. First and foremost, I want to thank Susan Phillips. Without her intense interest in Whitesbog history, her guidance, and her assistance, I doubt I would have ever undertaken this work. For my own personal desire to learn about the region, the people and the industries, I must credit all those volunteers who provided my first contact with Whitesbog. They made me feel like family, and so I kept coming back.

I can never sufficiently thank my mentors in Whitesbog and Pine Barrens history, specifically Ted Gordon, Mark Ehlenfeldt, and Rick Prickett, who shared their knowledge so liberally with me. I am also grateful to the Board of Directors of the Whitesbog Preservation Trust for allowing me such free access to archival materials. I would be remiss if I did not offer a hearty thank you to my sister-in-law, Carol, and my friend, Darla, who were so willing to be my first editors and who continually goaded me to move the manuscript forward. To Brenda Conner and Joe Darlington, thanks for always making family treasures and company records available to me. They were invaluable in enabling me to understand Elizabeth better, especially within the family dynamic.

I owe thanks to ever so many persons whom I contacted for personal or family recollections, archival data and background information, among them: Members of Grace Episcopal Church in Pemberton, Bob Reeves, Stephen Hutton, Jim Davis, Lynn Magyar Zwigard, as well as staff archivists at Drexel University, Hahnemann Hospital, and Rutgers University. Finally, I thank all those dear friends at Whitesbog and Emmaus who offered so much encouragement throughout this process.

Albertine Senske

With Eager Hands

Elizabeth C. White:
Whose Child is This?

It was the beginning of October 1871. Joseph Josiah White, affectionately known as J. J., was a reflective young man, and there was much to occupy his 25-year-old mind. The prior year had been eventful, a combination of highs and lows. He and his wife, Mary Anne "Minnie" Fenwick White, had published *Cranberry Culture* (1870), a guide to cranberry growing which met with much acclaim, J. J. supplying the text and Mary Anne, the illustrations. His Rake Pond cranberry bog was proving to be quite successful. To his great joy, he and his wife had welcomed their first daughter, Rebecca Merritt White. Unfortunately, their happiness was short-lived, as Rebecca died before reaching her first birthday. Now, once again, Minnie was only days away from giving birth to their second child. J. J. was experiencing anxiety and concern for his wife and his unborn child, but, at the same time, had a sense of anticipation and hope. If given the blessing of good health, the possibilities were endless. Whether boy or girl, this little one would be loved. He and his wife would do all in their power to help turn possibilities into realities.

Elizabeth Coleman White was born on October 5, 1871, at Fenwick Manor in New Lisbon, New Jersey. Minnie had returned to her family's home for her delivery, so doting parents and grandparents surrounded Elizabeth from her first day. As he wished and prayed for the best, did J. J. White considered the blessings that had already come into this child's life simply by being born into this family?

The history of the White family[6] in America began in 1675. Seeking the freedom to follow his Quaker beliefs and to keep his savings from government seizure, Christopher White (1642–1693) purchased one thousand acres of land in the New World from Sir John Fenwick.[7] While still residing in London, he signed "The Concessions and Agreements of the Proprietors, Freeholders, and Inhabitants of the Province of West Jersey in America," which became the initial fundamental law for West New Jersey. On June 28, 1677, Christopher White, his wife Hester, and son Josiah arrived in the village of Salem in West New Jersey Province, full of hope.[8] In England, Christopher had been a master carpenter. In America, in addition to prospering through his craft, he also became a successful farmer on the fertile banks of Alloway Creek. Christopher White gained the respect of his neighbors through his involvement in community affairs, even serving in the General Assembly.

Christopher left a goodly heritage, which his son, Josiah (1675–1713), in turn, maintained, improved, and left to his son, also named Josiah (1705–1780). In addition to farming, the younger Josiah had an interest in constructing dams, considering himself quite proficient in this pursuit. He was so sure of his ability to help farmers in the flood plain of the Alloway that he offered to build a dam with his own funds, seeking remuneration only if the dam remained intact for a year.

One day before the year was up, the dam "mysteriously" sprang a leak and so the farmers rendered no payment. Josiah's estate was gone and so was Josiah.[9] He moved from the area and re-established himself in Mount Holly, New Jersey, circa 1730.[10] There, like his grandfather Christopher, he began a new life.

Josiah White opened a fuller's business in Mount Holly, and, by the time he had been in the town twenty years, he was respected as a business leader and a man of high ideals.[11] Josiah and his wife Rebecca (Foster) had to wait eighteen years before they had a son who survived infancy: John (1747–1785). Josiah's expectation of having this son as a business partner and successor was not realized, since John was physically frail throughout his life and died at age 38.

John's sons, Josiah (1781–1850), and Joseph (1785–1827), carried on the White legacy of intelligence, ingenuity, and industriousness. Josiah was apprenticed to a hardware store proprietor in Philadelphia. In time, he bought out the owner and ran the store with his brother, Joseph. Josiah was a dreamer and a doer. Recognizing the imminent move toward industrialization and the subsequent need for steam power and improved methods for iron production, Josiah left Joseph to operate the hardware store while he pursued plans to transport anthracite coal from the mines of northeastern Pennsylvania to Philadelphia via natural and artificial waterways. Josiah White founded the Lehigh Coal and Navigation Company to accomplish this goal. At the same time, Joseph became a successful entrepreneur, establishing a coal distribution network with branches in multiple locations.

Joseph White went on to marry and raise a family. One of his sons, Barclay White (1821–1906), was the father of Joseph Josiah (J. J.) White (1846–1924), father of Elizabeth (1871–1954). In his youth, Barclay labored on a New Jersey farm called SHARON, which, at the time, belonged to Joseph Lamb, uncle to his future wife, Rebecca Merritt Lamb. In time, Barclay bought the property, situated between Jobstown and Juliustown, and raised his family here. Barclay and Rebecca had four sons: Howard, Joseph, George, and Barclay. Rebecca died days after giving birth to her last child. Faced with the daunting task of caring for four young boys, Barclay soon remarried. Together, he and Beulah Shreve had one son, Daniel.

Barclay was an innovator in his own right, experimenting early on with cranberry cultivation in an area known as Sim Place, about twenty-five miles from SHARON.[12] Also, following in his ancestors' footprints, Barclay became a respected member of the community. He was a devout member of the Quaker Meeting at Arney's Mount and passed on Quaker values to each of his sons. His reputation for fairness and honesty came to the attention of President Ulysses S. Grant, who appointed Barclay as Head of Indian Affairs for the Nebraska Territory. Following his return from the West, Barclay settled in Mount Holly, where he remained until his death in 1906.

Thus far, Elizabeth White's ancestors had endowed her with a legacy of high moral values, ingenuity, intellectual curiosity, industriousness, being community-minded, and the courage to forge new paths. She received no less from the Fenwick line.

Both Grandfather James Fenwick (1818–1882) and Grandmother Mary Anne Fenwick *née* Cashell (1825–1911) learned early in life how to deal with adversity. Each had been orphaned as very young children and raised by relatives. Both of Grandmother Fenwick's parents died before she was six months old. Responsibility for the baby fell to her mother's brother, Charles Thursby. There must have been considerable money in the Thursby family and possibly also in the Cashell family. When Uncle Thursby died, at the age of 27, a guardian, appointed to care for little Mary Cashell and her property, boarded the child with a woman in Trenton, New Jersey (and later with a Mrs. Coleman in Pemberton, New Jersey). The guardian supplied funds for the child's keep. When Mary Cashell was about sixteen, plans called for her to attend St. Mary's Hall in Burlington, New Jersey, one of the first schools in the county for the higher education of women. Before these plans could be put into effect, however, her guardian absconded with all of her available property.[13]

Grandfather James Fenwick received no such gift. He and Mary Anne were destined to make their own way through the work of their hands, he as a farmer, she as a homemaker. Fenwick supplied the workers at Hanover Furnace with produce from his farm. When the furnace closed, many of its workers followed the owner to Florence, New Jersey. Fenwick's customer base was suddenly decimated. Around this same time, some daring New Jersey farmers began to consider cranberries as a potential crop. James Fenwick became a fellow pioneer. From what he learned, he knew that the soil on his farm was unsuitable. He turned to his friend, Dr.

Pierson Coleman, for help.[14] Coleman owned a piece of land in Pemberton that appeared suitable and allowed Fenwick to establish an experimental bog. Encouraged by his success in this venture, James began to search for land on which to begin what he hoped would be a prosperous enterprise. Little did he know that his purchase of a 408-acre tract would spawn a legacy of respect, innovation, and prosperity.

The Early Years

Shortly after Elizabeth's birth, the White family moved back to SHARON and everyday life began. J. J. remained occupied with the Rake Pond bogs, Minnie with running the household, and Elizabeth with whatever keep babies busy. Within two years, the little family of three became four when J. J. and Minnie welcomed a new daughter into the world. Mary Fenwick White was born at SHARON in 1873. From the beginning, J. J. White had a loving relationship with each of his daughters. This is very evident in a letter that he wrote to three-year-old Elizabeth. At the time, Barclay White served as the head of Indian Affairs in Nebraska and resided in Omaha. In his absence, he had asked J. J. White to manage his affairs at home. From time to time, J. J. traveled to Nebraska both to visit his father and to conduct business. On one such visit he penned the following:

My Dear Little Lizzie—

Although I am about fifteen hundred miles from home I often think of Mother and thee and dear little chick and wish I could have you on my lap all at once.

The weather has been very cold out here and the ice on the Missouri River is more than two feet thick and so strong that it makes a very good bridge for horses to cross on. Uncle Dan lives here and he has so many whiskers on his face that thee can scarcely know him. I slept with him last night and think he would be a pretty good bed-fellow if he only had a longer bed.

Take good care of little sister while I am away and then I will be sure to kiss thee when I come home.

From thy dear father.   J. W.[15]

In July 1873, the Fenwick family suffered a tragic loss when their only son, Thane, Minnie's brother, died quite suddenly from complications of typhoid fever. Thane had not followed in his father's footsteps. He preferred a career in retail to one in agriculture. Grief overtook the family, so J. J. and Minnie made the decision to leave SHARON and, at least temporarily, move to New Lisbon to offer support and comfort in this difficult period.

Elizabeth grew especially close to Grandfather Fenwick. On one occasion, he surprised her with two gifts, a colorful rocking horse and a pitcher plant. Later in life, Elizabeth would write about that day and the gift of the "long stemmed dark red flowers of the Pitcher Plant" which came from "the bog" where Grandfather Fenwick had started the culture of cranberries in 1857. She continues,

> Many were the treasures that came to that little grand-daughter from "the bog": great mats of Pixie Moss thickly dotted with pink which opened into starry white flowers; spicy red tea berries, a delight to the eye and so good to eat; a tiny turtle perhaps, or a beautiful stem of Tiger Lilies.[16]

Fenwick also imbued Elizabeth with respect for others. While riding in a buggy one day, Elizabeth and her grandfather passed the home of an elderly gentleman who had been a customer of Fenwick when he supplied the workers at Hanover Furnace with fresh produce. Fenwick stopped to greet the man. The deference and respect her grandfather showed toward this individual made an impression on Elizabeth that would last her lifetime.

Many other childhood memories stayed with Elizabeth, sometimes in vivid detail. While residing in New Lisbon, J. J. White served as Superintendent of the First Day School at the old Arneys Mount Friends Meeting House, where he and his brothers had worshiped for years. Elizabeth recalls,

> Father sometimes took me with him on these Sunday trips. We went in the buggy drawn by Frank, the old light colored horse, somewhere between cream color and bay. I was too small to be left with the other children and sat beside Father on the facing bench in front of the board propped up by a stick which served as a desk . . . One day my little stuck out feet hit the prop and—bang—down fell the desk and its burden. One of the good Friends, in her straight bonnet, later put her kindly hand on my abashed head with its dark brown hair and assured me she knew I hadn't meant to. I certainly hadn't.[17]

That last sentence makes one think she was still embarrassed by the memory years later.

J. J. White belonged to a family steeped in the Quaker tradition. He remained a Friend throughout his life and offered this way of life to his daughters. Mary Anne Fenwick, Elizabeth's grandmother, had been raised in the Episcopal Church; her father had served as the first warden in Grace Episcopal Church in Pemberton. Grandfather James Fenwick had, at different times in his life, belonged to the Roman Catholic Church and to a Quaker meeting prior to becoming a member of Grace Episcopal Church.

The White daughters became involved in the parish life of Grace Episcopal. Mary and Beulah played the organ and taught Sunday School. Elizabeth helped at parish functions as she could, depending on her duties at the bog. The girls also accompanied J. J. to Meeting. The moral principles and Christian values by which they lived seemed more important to this family than the church they attended.

J. J. White was a man of great intellectual curiosity. He maintained a keen interest in many different fields of study and, at some point in his life, he was drawn to mechanical engineering. Never having studied in the field, although he spent a year at the Polytechnic Institute of Pennsylvania, he nonetheless sought employment at the H. B. Smith Machine Company in Smithville. This move answered two needs: it provided him with engineering training and it supplemented his income from the Rake Pond Bog. A daily trip from New Lisbon was out of the question. J. J. found lodging at Smithville during the week, returning to Fenwick Manor by train on Saturday afternoon. Elizabeth writes,

> I remember my nose pressed against the window waiting impatiently for his reappearance and soon two

tall men would appear walking up the hill. The second was "Uncle" John Salter, mother's second cousin.[18]

J. J. White proved a quick learner. After just two years, Smith promoted him to supervisor and the family moved to Smithville. It was here that Mary Fenwick White gave birth to a son, Joseph, who lived only a very short time, as well as a daughter, Beulah Sansom White. The Whites remained in Smithville until about 1881, when J. J. became supervisor of selling machinery for H. B. Smith in Philadelphia. That promotion, and the imminent death of James Fenwick, precipitated the move back to New Lisbon, where the last child to survive, Anne Pierson White, was born. For the next forty years, Elizabeth would call Fenwick Manor "home." She would have been ten years old at the time of her grandfather's death.

Prior to his death in 1882, Fenwick had appointed J. J. White executor of his will and manager of his cranberry farm in the pines. White commuted daily between New Lisbon and his full-time employment in Philadelphia. It was on Saturday that he devoted his energies to managing the Fenwick cranberry business. Almost sixty years later, in an address at the annual convention of the American Cranberry Growers' Association, Elizabeth White reminisced:

> . . . on Saturdays he [her father] drove eastward the seven long, sandy miles to "the bog," taking a lunch and nearly always one or more of his four little girls. Seldom did I miss a trip.[19]

These weekly excursions were the beginning of her agricultural lessons. She eavesdropped on the conversations between J. J. and the farm superintendent. If the discussion was clearly over her head, she amused herself until it was time for the trip home. This was also the beginning of Elizabeth's becoming the son J. J. White never had.

A Love of Learning

Elizabeth White's interest in education stemmed from her own experience. All through her formative years, her family provided Elizabeth with a variety of learning experiences. She attended the local school, received homeschooling for a time, then was sent to Friends Central in Philadelphia to complete high school. After graduation, Elizabeth attended Drexel College extension classes, where she learned of cultural subjects through lectures, plays, and musical performances. Her grandfather, father, and others tutored her in all things horticultural. One has only to look at her accomplishments to know that she took advantage of and nurtured each of these opportunities. What she didn't learn formally, she discovered through reading. The desire to learn and to help others learn remained a passion throughout her life.

Formal records do not exist to identify exactly the type of education Elizabeth received in her early years. Because the White family experienced several moves between 1873 and 1882, it is most probable that home-schooling was the first method of education. From notations in the diary of Beulah White, Elizabeth's sister, the girls clearly had tutors for various subjects. Elizabeth herself verified that she attended the local school in New Lisbon. "For a time I attended the public school near my home with the other piney children."[20] When White was sixteen years old, she, together with her fourteen-year-old sister, Mary, boarded at Friends Central to complete high school. At the time, the school stood on Race Street in the heart of Philadelphia.

J. J. White's grandfather, Joseph, had set in motion the family tradition of attending Quaker School. Joseph (1785–1827) did not have the opportunity. His father, John White (1747–1785), had been sickly and died of consumption (tuberculosis) at the age of 38. Joseph's mother, Rebecca Powell White, assumed control of the family's fuller business in Mount Holly and Joseph worked side by side with his mother until he entered into a partnership with his brother, Josiah, in operating a hardware store in Philadelphia. Joseph proved to be an astute businessman and entrepreneur. His location in a metropolitan area presented possibilities, not only for him, but also for his children. Barclay White, a son of Joseph, attended Westtown School, a day's ride west of Philadelphia, as did Barclay's own son, J. J. White.

The tradition continued with J. J. White's daughters. When she turned sixteen, Elizabeth, and her sister, Mary, began attending Friends Central School in Philadelphia. The year 1888 proved to be a milestone year for these two White daughters, a kind of "coming out." On Easter Sunday they were baptized, becoming members of Grace Episcopal Church and, in September, they moved away from the familiarity and comfort of home. J. J. traveled to the city every day for work. It is possible that his daughters made the trip with him. It is just as likely that they boarded with another family that had students attending the school. This was a normal practice among the Quaker community. J. J. and Minnie would have made sure their daughters were prepared to join students who may have been part of the system for several years. Home schooling undoubtedly included hired tutors.

Upon entering school, even though of different ages, Mary and Elizabeth attended the same classes. Friends Central offered four tracks: classical, scientific, literary, and irregular. The White girls followed the literary curriculum. Their classes included the usual subjects like reading, arithmetic, algebra, literature, composition and orthography.[21] From school records, the only difference in the girls' schedules was that Mary studied French while Elizabeth received drawing instruction. Elizabeth's formal study of bookkeeping would come into play almost thirty years later when she prepared to assume keeping financial records for J. J. White, Inc., replacing her sister, Beulah, as the latter readied for marriage and a move to Lansdowne, Pennsylvania.[22]

During their two years at Friends, Mary always received a higher grade in orthography but, by and large, they performed quite similarly. Both young ladies excelled in geology, Elizabeth earning a perfect score in one marking period. Both girls did well, but overall, Mary's grades were slightly higher than Elizabeth's. It seems ironic that Mary would outperform Elizabeth in rhetoric when, in later life, Elizabeth would become an excellent orator. After graduating in June 1890, the White girls kept in touch with classmates. They attended class reunions and even hosted the event both at New Lisbon and, later, at SUNINGIVE (1935).

What Elizabeth did between June 1890 and September 1893 is unclear. In the Whitesbog archives, there is a simple, unsigned biographical sketch of Elizabeth, dated 1953. It is so different in content from the other accounts of her life and so factually accurate, that the only logical conclusion is that Elizabeth herself wrote it. This would be consistent with Quaker practice to prepare material that could be used in an obituary. J. J. White did this in 1914, calling the piece "Cranberry Culture," not to be confused with his agricultural treatise written in 1870. The section of the Elizabeth White document that speaks of education after Friends Central reads: "During the several succeeding years there were odd terms at Drexel Institute, Philadelphia, Pa., in English, Chemistry etc."[23] Traditional lore would have the "et cetera" to be dressmaking and millinery, first aid, and photography. One of these claims is correct; one is false, and one is still a question mark. A few words about Drexel might be helpful before examining these claims.

By the late nineteenth century, the pace of technological change in America demanded new models of higher education. Legendary financier and philanthropist Anthony J. Drexel answered that call in 1891 when he opened the Drexel Institute of Art, Science, and Industry at 32nd and Chestnut streets in Philadelphia. The goal of Drexel was to prepare students for careers in new industries. Whereas, heretofore, college had been the exclusive stronghold of upper-class men studying for the ministry, the law, or medicine, Drexel's ideals would make a much broader kind of education available without restrictions based on race, gender, or socioeconomic status. This revolutionary concept must have appealed greatly to both J. J. and Elizabeth White.

Originally a non-degree-granting institution, Drexel conferred a certificate upon completion of its two-year program. When official classes began in 1892, the institute offered a variety of courses in subjects ranging from art and illustration, mechanical arts, domestic arts and sciences, commerce and finance, and teacher training. Basics such as English composition were part of the core curriculum.

So, what courses did Elizabeth take while attending Drexel Institute? The Archives at Drexel are the primary source of information. Drexel's archivist and the author both conducted research to answer this question. Unfortunately, according to Drexel, records are sketchy at best for intermittent students.

Dress Making and Millinery: Elizabeth took a class in this subject in February 1894. She received ratings of good or very good in specific aspects such as folding, binding, trimming and an excellent grade on the written examination. Photography: No record was found to support this claim. That Miss White studied photography is evident from a series of photos that are part of the Whitesbog archives. They appear to be part of a portfolio, all matted identically and identified on the back with Elizabeth's full name and address. For Elizabeth to have taken this subject at Drexel, she would have had to have done so in 1892 since, according to Drexel historians Edward D. McDonald and Edward M. Hinton, the school only offered photography in the first year, after which it was discontinued due to the poor quality of the class. It was reintroduced at a later point in time. So, it is possible that Elizabeth took that first-year class. However, returning to the previously mentioned biographical sketch, the mention of chemistry prompts questions.

An examination of Drexel syllabi from the early years reveals a clue. One of the chemistry classes concentrated on silver, particularly as it dealt with photography. In the 1880s and 1890s, silver gelatin papers for photography were the most widely used both by amateurs and professionals. After about 1890, collodion, platinum, and, steadily declining in popularity, albumen prints were also made. Elizabeth may have developed her own films. We do know that she made her own prints as Beulah, writing in her diary, recounts assisting Elizabeth with making prints of the pictures taken on their European trip.

First Aid: Elizabeth White did not study first aid at Drexel. In a letter to Owen Lovejoy, Secretary General of the National Child Labor Committee, J. J. White states:

> The growers are not unmindful of the welfare of their pickers; for instance, the daughter of one of the largest growers [Elizabeth] has for the last 12 years given his pickers first aid when sick or injured, a duty for which she especially qualified herself at one of the leading Philadelphia hospitals.[24]

This would have placed Elizabeth's training in the late 1890s. At the time, the major hospitals included Hahnemann, Women's Medical,[25] and Pennsylvania (not connected to the University). Each had a Nursing

School associated with it. Research into the archives of all three failed to identify any records for White. She most likely took classes only during the winter months when she was not engaged in active cranberry farming and she would have been interested only in what she needed to assist the farmworkers, not the entire nursing curriculum. Once again, the archivists indicated that it was not customary to retain records for part-time students. Although Drexel was the last stop in her formal education, Elizabeth White enjoyed a lifetime of learning. She immersed herself in literature on a variety of subjects, chief of which was agriculture. She continuously scanned the publications of the USDA for relevant topics. She also subscribed to magazines on horticulture and botany. Social justice was another concern dear to her heart, as well as a topic of study.

Because she treasured her own education so much, Elizabeth White wanted others to have the same opportunity. As a teenage girl continuously expanding her own knowledge base, she would not have been able to imagine the educational impact she would have on so many lives and in so many ways.

Elizabeth C. White the Horticulturist:
Cranberries 101

From 1857 to the present, Whitesbog has served primarily as a cranberry farm. The core property belonged to James Fenwick. Fenwick died in 1882, leaving the management of the land to his son-in-law, J. J. White. During the week, J. J. commuted to Philadelphia, where he managed a branch of H. B. Smith, Inc., a company that specialized in belt-driven woodworking machinery, but each Saturday he traveled to Fenwick's bog to meet and plan with the farm superintendent. For the next thirty years, White was a faithful steward of Fenwick's enterprise while also planning for the future by surrounding the original farm with his own land acquisitions and cranberry business.

When Mary E. Cashell Fenwick passed away in 1911, she bequeathed the Fenwick portion to her daughter, Mary Anne White. Less than a year later, on March 6, 1912, deeds drawn unified the various parcels into one property. Then, on April 1, 1912, Joseph J. White, Inc., began to conduct business as a new company.[26] This was truly a family business. Each of J. J. and Minnie's daughters received shares and was free to voice her opinion and cast an independent vote at regular company meetings. The girls were well qualified to do this because, from the beginning, their father had shared ongoing bog activity and long-range plans with his family.

By the time J. J. White incorporated his farming operation, Elizabeth had been working at the bog for more than eighteen years. From the beginning, she was well acquainted with the running of the farm. As a child, she seldom missed accompanying her father on his weekly visit to the bogs. She listened to his instructions to the superintendent and absorbed what she could at any given age. This fascination with cranberry culture and farming methodology continued during Elizabeth's entire life. Sometime in the early 1890s, she accompanied her father on a sea voyage to New England in search of the best Howe cranberry vines to bring back and plant in New Jersey.[27] They visited many bogs and met with A. D. Makepeace, one of Massachusetts' premier cranberry growers. Of this encounter, Elizabeth writes: "That evening the girl listened and absorbed much of the slow, quiet exchange of thoughts of the two big cranberry men."[28] Finally, in 1893, J. J. White decided his daughter was ready to assume formal duties in the family business, just in time for the cranberry harvest.

Early on September 1—not more than six o'clock a.m.—Elizabeth left New Lisbon farm in the company of her father and made the journey to the bogs. She was a month shy of her twenty-second birthday. The buggy in which they traveled carried the household and personal items that the young woman would require over the course of the next several weeks. Elizabeth's home away from home would be a small ten by twelve building located a short distance from the home of Bill Hance, then the bog superintendent. Here, she stored her clothes, food, and whatever personal items or furnishings she had brought.[29]

Minnie White made sure that Elizabeth would be well-fed during the week. She had a small three-burner oil stove on which to prepare her meals. For the first time, Elizabeth was on her own. From some notes in family papers, however, it appears that her parents held concerns for her safety at night, so she slept in the superintendent's house. Her bedroom there had a bedstead and mattress, but she brought all the bedding from New Lisbon. It is unknown how long these sleeping arrangements remained intact, but that little cabin served as Elizabeth's harvest home for many years to come. Each week, the routine remained the same unless altered by unforeseen difficulties on the bogs. On Saturday afternoon, Elizabeth would pack the buggy with soiled clothes and linens and leftover food and head home to spend Sunday with the family. Then, Sunday evening or early Monday morning, the buggy would be reloaded, and the faithful horse, Daisy, would make the trip to the bog to begin a new week.[30]

Over the years, Elizabeth assumed many responsibilities in working on the cranberry bogs. The first was inspecting the pickers' baskets for the quantity and quality of the product and then marking their payment tickets. As she explained to Gove Hambridge, "The payroll depended on these tickets and we found them a source of graft and irregularity on the part of the foreman; so, my father decided to let me handle them."[31] The crop in 1893 proved a bountiful one. About 200 men, women, and children arrived on that first day to begin the picking.

Some had come prepared to stay. These workers found shelter in rude shacks available for that purpose. Others came from nearby and worked on a day laborer basis, as the need or their inclination dictated. The Whites would see the demographics of their labor base change dramatically as the cranberry farm expanded and thus required a larger, more stable, workforce. The superintendent recruited Italian immigrants from Philadelphia, sometimes as many as four to five hundred, who then came to Whitesbog and remained for the entire season. The increase in the number of pickers also changed Elizabeth's routine and responsibilities somewhat. No longer did she arrive on the first day of harvest. She and her sister Beulah met the pickers the day before so that work could begin promptly on day one. Beulah distributed tickets while Elizabeth handed out picking baskets. Both items received an identifying number assigned to each officially recognized employee. Elizabeth also trained others to assist her in inspecting baskets and marking the pickers' tickets. Frequently, these were native "Pineys," rather than migrant laborers.[32]

At first, the routine during harvest was to complete all the picking and then to sort and ship. Initially, each grower was responsible for selling his own berries. Then, in 1895, J. J. White, the elder Theodore Budd, Richard Harrison, and some large growers from New England, like Makepeace, united to form a marketing company called Growers Cranberry Company and hired Charles Wilkinson to sell the berries of the members under their individual brands. The motto of the new company was "Hand assorted and uniformly packed."

Elizabeth tells us that her first duty in the sorting house was to stamp this motto onto each barrel.[33] In 1904, J. J. added his newly acquired "White Star" trademark to the labeling process. By 1907, in an effort to gain an advantage from being one of the first shippers to market, J. J. began sorting and shipping very shortly after picking began, thereby changing the original routine. Elizabeth's sister Mary supervised the sorting process, while Elizabeth continued to oversee the picking and, ultimately, the shipping. Not to be left out, Beulah White tracked the number of bushels shipped in her role as company treasurer.

While Elizabeth White began her work on the farm during the harvest season, she soon was there on a full-time basis. She performed many other tasks required to ensure a good crop. She described her role on several occasions. In a document prepared as historical background for a suit Joseph J. White, Inc., brought against Beaver Dam Cranberry Company, she wrote the following:

> It was my Father's habit during such seasons to spend much time investigating the possibilities of future improvements at Whitesbog and then to sit with me where I was receiving berries at the side of the bog to talk over his plans. After the picking season was over it was his custom to take me to see the places where he planned to build dams or cut ditches.[34]

She reiterated her position on the farm to Eleanor Morton, biographer of Josiah White (1781–1850), who recorded: "All daughters helped in the business, but it was Elizabeth who took special interest in the building of dams, the management of the interlocking water system, the development of the bogs, and all her father's plans."[35] The Whites soon learned that insects such as girdler moths and army worms could decimate their crop. At first, not knowing the problems they faced, Elizabeth gathered several of the destructive insects and sent them off to Dr. John Smith, the state entomologist.

Over the years, Elizabeth learned that cranberry farming involved much more than just growing the berries. Marketing issues, legal restraints, cooperation with other growers, and the constant necessity to search for more productive and economical methods of doing business all played a part. J. J. White maintained involvement in all these aspects and Elizabeth White was his constant companion along the way.

Because of her intimate role at the Fenwick/White cranberry operation, Elizabeth may have initially assumed that she would succeed her father at its helm. At least that is the oral tradition. We know from history that this did not occur. One can only speculate why J. J. White chose an alternate route. Although he was progressive in so many ways, J. J. may have been traditional enough to opt for the norm of men running the business. Whatever the reason, in the middle of 1910, he approached his son-in-law about coming to work at the farm. At the time, Franklin S. Chambers, husband of the Whites' youngest daughter, Anne, was an engineer at Parker Boiler Company in Philadelphia. Chambers had no agricultural experience; he graduated from the University of Pennsylvania in 1904 with a degree in mechanical engineering. Still, he was a bright young man and appears to be have been willing to learn. Chambers came to the farm primarily in the capacity of engineer; over the course of time, however, whether by J. J.'s design or as a happy byproduct, he became an excellent cranberry man.

Frank Chambers began his internship at Joseph J. White, Inc., in January 1911. Putting all personal feelings aside, Elizabeth White served as his teacher and mentor in the field training process in conjunction with Ivins Hornor, then the superintendent. In addition to introducing Chambers to the normal tasks and maintenance associated with running the farm, Elizabeth and Frank took on a major improvement project—a new spraying system for the bogs. Chambers also became involved in the financial aspects of the company and took charge of the farm expenses under the guidance of Beulah White while she retained all the personnel accounts. Ordinarily, J. J. White would have had a greater hands-on role in Frank Chambers' education, but 1911 proved to be an exceptionally difficult year for White, medically speaking. It is a great testimony to J. J.'s confidence in his daughters' abilities that he entrusted the task to them.

J. J. White always sought to improve his own personal business enterprises and the business of New Jersey's cranberry industry. He returned from a trip to California in 1904 with reports of that state's citrus fruit cooperatives and some ideas of how the concept could be adapted to the cranberry market. In April of that year, he addressed fellow growers, pointing out their alacrity to increase land and production without spending the same energy to increase market demand. White tried to make his colleagues more aware of their current practices of independent marketing, which resulted in uneven distribution and price fluctuation. However, New Jersey growers were cautious. Talks did not generate any action until 1907, when the members of Growers Cranberry Company agreed to consider merging with the Chicago-based National Fruit Exchange, the selling arm for Wisconsin, New England, and New Jersey farmers.

Now began another period of talking, arguing, disagreeing and even dishonorable actions. J. J. White, representing Growers Cranberry Company, and Judge John Gaynor, a Wisconsin farmer speaking on behalf of the National Fruit Exchange, did their best to steer the participants on a productive course of action. After four years of this behavior, J. J. was ready to abandon all efforts. Finally, a successful vote occurred, giving birth to the American Cranberry Exchange.

White, however, did not fare so well. The day after the vote, he collapsed with what his daughter Beulah termed a heart attack. Whatever the actual diagnosis, his doctor relegated J. J. White to rest and recuperation for the next six months. Her father's health-imposed inactivity placed additional responsibility on Elizabeth. Although the decision to consolidate had been made, many open issues remained to be resolved before a working organization came into being. Retaining private labels was of major concern. J. J. White was unable to participate in these discussions. He sent Elizabeth to represent his position, knowing that she had the knowledge and the ability, as well as the respect of the other participants. Ultimately, J. J. White agreed to not using private brands and gave up his White Star trademark. Thirty years later, Elizabeth would share the emotions of this experience with the members of the Cranberry Association.

> After spending many seasons supervising the cleaning and shipping of our cranberries, helping to build up the reputation of the White Star Brand, it was hard, very hard, to abandon it and work for the cooperative Eatmor brand. I long since came to realize how wise father was in making that change and words are not adequate to express my appreciation of the leadership of A. U. Chaney and the effectiveness of his work in stabilizing the market and developing advertising and the cooperative spirit in general.[36]

As if the turmoil of forming a new cooperative wasn't stressful enough, in 1911, the American Cranberry Growers Association[37] faced national scrutiny after being singled out by the National Child Labor Committee (NCLC), a private charity based in New York. In December 1910, the NCLC distributed a public information pamphlet denouncing the horrors of child labor on New Jersey cranberry bogs. This was followed in 1911 with a full-blown article in the group's official publication, *The Survey*. Many pictures (about one-third taken at Whitesbog) taken by Lewis Hine, a name now almost synonymous with child labor, accompanied the exposé. Long hours and unhealthy picking conditions, educational deprivation, and sub-standard living quarters comprised some of injustices attributed to the farmers. Members turned to J. J. White for guidance.

Early in January, White wrote to NCLC Secretary, Owen Lovejoy, defending both himself and his fellow growers. Then came the final push for the co-op and J. J. White's collapse. It would be up to someone else to continue the fight. Frank Chambers immediately addressed the charges that numerous medical problems resulted from children's time on the bogs. He approached the local doctors who attended the pickers during the harvest and received exonerating testimonials. Once again, however, it was Elizabeth who stepped into her father's shoes and negotiated on the broader level. For her first act, she wrote to Jane Addams of Hull House who, in addition to serving on the NCLC Board of Trustees, had created her own programs in Chicago addressing the needs of women and children.

Elizabeth would continue defending the growers for several years to come. She would also attempt to take an honest appraisal of the situation and to improve conditions where they appeared below par. Her involvement in all aspects of the migrant workers' life would be a continuum for most of her life.

As White spoke out on their behalf, the members of the American Cranberry Growers Association grew in their respect for her. According to the Proceedings of the Association's Fortieth Annual Convention in 1909, members already considered Elizabeth "an expert in cranberry culture." This opinion suggests she had participated in the Association's meetings on a regular basis, probably since her official involvement in bog business, beginning in 1893. It was not until 1912, however, that the association offered her a membership, making history by being the first woman to achieve this milestone.[38] The distinction was repeated eighteen years later when, in 1930, Elizabeth became the first woman president of the Association. At the Annual Convention in August 1929, she delivered a speech to the members that exemplified her forward-thinking attitude. Continuing a theme that she had initiated at the Association's annual meeting the previous January, she took advantage of the expanded audience to urge growers to consider the importance of persistent searching for improved cranberry varieties. She reminded them of the significance that Abel Makepeace placed on selecting the best vines those many years before, when the industry was in its infancy. Elizabeth's forward-thinking and concern for the future is exemplified in her reasoning for varietal experimentation.

> Today, however, there is urgent need of something better. The Howes are exceedingly susceptible to the false blossom disease, and have cooking qualities that make them undesirable for canning, which, it appears, is destined to play so important a role in the future of the cranberry industry.[39]

Elizabeth reminded the growers that in January she had shared with those present at the meeting the experimentation she herself had begun, using her blueberry experience; she now reported what appeared to be some success. "I feel hopeful as to the outcome of this voyage." Elizabeth may have been optimistic, but she was also realistic. She knew it was a daunting challenge for farmers who felt comfortable with the plants and product that had served them well for many years.

> Yes, I know what you are thinking. It will be a slow process covering so many years as to be almost hopeless. Not so long ago I thought so too. But after having seen and intimately known what has been accomplished with blueberry varieties in less than twenty years, I feel that plants are as clay in the hands of the potter, and that skill in pottering with cranberry vines will grow as we work on the job.[40]

Just how strong a role she played in the Cranberry Growers Association becomes clear from A. J. Rider, long-time secretary of the group, upon its fiftieth anniversary. When recounting the outstanding achievements of several members over the years, he states the following:

> It is time to pass out a few bouquets to the worthy ones . . . And then there is our talented and most useful member, Miss Elizabeth White, who has been styled the best Cranberry man in New Jersey, say nothing of her achievement in blueberry culture. I wish I had two for her.[41]

Elizabeth was not afraid to express her opinion and her experience, being sure to credit Frank Chambers as appropriate, since she worked closely with her father and brother-in-law to expand and improve the farm.

It was not only the local organization that recognized her ability and contributions. During the long process of forming the cranberry cooperative, many growers in New Jersey and New England resented the influence and leadership of Arthur Chaney, the midwest marketer being proposed to become the head of the American Cranberry Exchange. J. J. White recognized Chaney's expertise in reading the marketplace and developing advertising strategies. He urged his neighbors to use Chaney, instead of opposing him. Elizabeth took notice, and, through the years, she and Chaney developed a close working relationship.

The Growers versus Chaney rift would replay itself in Elizabeth White's lifetime. This second disagreement occurred between the American Cranberry Exchange and Cranberry Canners Inc. Marcus Urann, a Massachusetts grower, possessed abilities similar to Chaney to read and to anticipate, not the fruit market, but the public's food taste. Cranberry sauce had been in people's diets since the 1700s. Urann conceived the idea to prepare it, can it, and offer it as a year-round commodity, thus extending the selling period and finding a way to use the smaller, non-marketable berries. The concept ushered in the birth of Ocean Spray Cranberry Cooperative. At the same time, John Makepeace in Massachusetts and Elizabeth Lee in New Jersey had begun their own canning businesses. In 1930, the three merged to form Cranberry Canners, Inc. To avoid antitrust prosecution, the company formed as a cooperative. Now growers had to deal with two co-ops: one for the fresh fruit market and the other to handle fruit to be used in processed food.

Elizabeth, following in J. J.'s footsteps, analyzed Marcus Urann as a man and as a business leader. She liked what she saw, but not everyone shared her opinion. Many mistrusted Urann, as they had Chaney before him, resulting in the spreading of lies and discontent. Then came the growing season of 1937, which produced a bumper crop in every part of the country. The market became saturated with fresh berries, and, in the middle of the selling period, a general business depression occurred. Prices dropped with no orders coming in; 200,000 barrels of fresh fruit sat in storage. Arthur Chaney tried his best to sell the surplus at $7 a barrel. Brokers laughed, saying they would soon be able to buy the same berries for $2 a barrel. Then Marcus Urann stepped in and began to buy the excess fruit.

To do so, Cranberry Canners took out a one-million-dollar loan. By the time Urann was finished, an extra three million dollars went into the pockets of the growers. Members of the Cranberry Exchange breathed a sigh of relief and then went on with business as usual. Urann received no publicity for what he had accomplished for the industry, so Elizabeth felt compelled to act. In 1940, she wrote an animated letter of complaint to Clarence Hall, founder and editor-in-chief of *Cranberries* magazine, who published the letter in its entirety in the April issue. After recounting Urann's deeds, Elizabeth, in completely uncharacteristic exuberance, exclaimed: "Oh!! Boy!! What Courage!! What a Job!!"

Elizabeth and Urann exchanged many letters over the years. While they primarily concerned business, personal information often found its way into the content. Urann expressed keen interest in a series of letters between James Fenwick and his cousin that had recently come into White's possession. Elizabeth promised him a copy when she had finished organizing the manuscripts. On occasion, Urann sought his friend's counsel when attempting to assess the mindset of New Jersey growers, particularly relative to consolidating the cooperatives that were handling processed and fresh cranberries. Urann also asked Elizabeth's opinion of two candidates for a position in Cranberry Canners. He favored one of the young men while the other, Edward Lipman, was Elizabeth's preference. Marcus Urann went with his choice, but five years later, when he needed a Director of New Jersey Growers Relations, Lipman got the job.

By the time Edward Lipman joined Cranberry Canners, Inc., in 1945, Elizabeth White was 75 years old and had been involved in the family's cranberry venture for over fifty years. She had both witnessed and participated in good times and bad: boon harvests and lean yields, a labor strike, war years with sparse labor forces, and experimentation and innovations in planting and harvesting methods. She, as well as Frank Chambers and the other members of Joseph J. White, Inc., had served the Company well, but now were tired and aging.

Hope for the Company's future now lay with Joseph Darlington, son of Beulah White Darlington. This hope was never fully realized. In 1948, Joe died tragically in an airplane accident. By the time of Darlington's demise, Frank Chambers had also passed on and no one stood in the wings, ready to assume management of the farm. Finally, Joseph's brother, Thomas, agreed to accept the position. Once again, Elizabeth saw Whitesbog come to the fore as Tom Darlington developed a new mechanical dry harvester and assumed his place as a leader in the American Cranberry Growers' Association. Joseph J. White, Inc., under the direction of Tom's son Joseph Darlington, continues to thrive and to serve the New Jersey cranberry industry.

An Adventure in Blue

By 1900, Elizabeth White had fully immersed herself in the overall growth and financial well-being of the farm. After beginning her cranberry career as picking supervisor, she moved on to running the packing and shipping operation. In the off-season, she frequently participated in bog development and maintenance. Elizabeth White became her father's confidante in planning for the future. The need for a second, backup crop was evident to both. They discussed the possibility of cultivating the wild blueberries that grew in abundance in the region and the frustration of not being able to take advantage of the situation.

> We had acres of land that could not be used for cranberries because it could not be flooded—even though there was water of waste after it had been used for irrigating the cranberries. We needed to stabilize our work force with work for the slack seasons; and we needed another income crop before the last months of the year, when our cranberries were harvested. Also a second crop might succeed in an off-year for cranberries. We knew the need of all fruit growers for a uniform high-grade fruit. Neighborhood farmer tradition said that "Huckleberries"[42] could not be cultivated. We did not know how to begin.[43]

Little did the Whites know that someone else held an interest in the "huckleberries" that thrived in and around the many bogs of the Pine Barrens. Frederick Vernon Coville was born March 23, 1867, in Preston, New York, to bank director Joseph Coville and his wife, Lydia. Frederick did not follow in his father's footsteps. He graduated from Cornell University in 1887 and obtained a position as a botanist with the United States Department of Agriculture the following year. Coville participated in the 1891 Death Valley Expedition led by Merriam and Palmer. At the end of the project, Coville published *Botany of the Death Valley Expedition* (1893), an impressive work on desert plants. This success may have contributed to his being named Chief Botanist at the USDA in 1893.

When the USDA established its Bureau of Plant Industries in 1901, Coville became head of the Office of Botanical Investigations and Experiments. He continued to travel in the western states, studying the plant life of the area. Summers, however, he spent with his wife Elizabeth and their children, Stanley, Katharine, Cabot, and Frederick, in rural areas of New England. In 1905, a friend told him of a farm for sale near Greenfield, New Hampshire, and, in May of that year, the Covilles bought the forty-acre property.

Coville soon discovered an abundance of wild blueberry bushes, both the highbush and lowbush varieties, growing in the fields surrounding the farm. By 1906, he had become sufficiently intrigued to begin a study of blueberry culture. He, along with the Whites, knew that previous attempts to propagate the plants had generally proven unsuccessful; he was determined to find out *why*. In a handwritten note, Coville recounts, "In the summer of 1906 some fresh blueberries from Greenfield picked by Katharine were turned over to Mr. G. [George] W. Oliver, who successfully grew seedlings from them, which were potted and finally sent to the Arlington Farm."[44] When he returned to Greenfield in 1908, Coville had almost 200 seedlings from the hothouses in Washington as a base for experimentation. It was also during that summer that Coville selected the blueberry bush that would provide the parentage for much of his experimentation.

> The parent of the seedlings of 1908 was a bush of *Vaccinium corymbosum* selected at Greenfield, NH, in July 1908, after three years of cursory observation in the mountains of southern New Hampshire and three weeks of diligent search in the summer of 1908. The bush grew at an elevation of 950 feet above the sea. . . . It was about 7 feet in height and the largest of the stems was about two inches in diameter. . . . The berries were of large size, reaching a diameter of over half an inch. . . . The only unfavorable feature was the lateness in the maturity of its berries.[45]

Coville named this plant 'Brooks' in honor of his neighbor, Fred Brooks, in whose field he found the bush. Between 1907 and 1910, Coville conducted myriad experiments that ultimately allowed him to determine several key factors in blueberry culture. Blueberries require a moist, but not wet soil with low pH; they also have a low nutrient requirement and require winter chilling. In addition, he developed propagation procedures through cuttings, grafting, and budding. Coville was ready to share his findings with the agricultural community in a treatise entitled "Experiments in Blueberry Culture." The USDA published it as Bulletin 193, listing it in their November 15, 1910, catalog.

Elizabeth White routinely checked the catalog for information that could be beneficial to their cranberry operation. When she saw the entry about blueberries, her heart must have beat a little faster and her hope must have risen, even if cautiously. She immediately sent for the publication and her hopes were not disappointed. As she came to the end of Coville's work, Elizabeth knew that the author understood the farmers' dilemma.

> These plants differ in their soil requirements so fundamentally from all our common cultivated crops that it is useless to expect to succeed with their culture without a thorough understanding of the principles that govern their growth.[46]

Father and daughter must have held many discussions throughout December 1910 regarding the implications that Coville's work might have on their own business. Could they play a role in this agricultural breakthrough? Should they get involved so early or wait for Coville to make further inroads? Did they even have the personnel to get involved?

J. J. was deeply enmeshed in attempting to establish a national cranberry cooperative, an initiative that was long, drawn-out, and enervating. Franklin Chambers was just coming onboard the Fenwick/White Farm operations. His apprenticeship would be time-consuming and intense and would fall, in great part, on Elizabeth. Additional workers would probably need to be hired, which would cut into the profitability for White's portion of the farm. Frederick Coville was a scientist. Simplistically put, his concern was "What makes this plant grow and thrive?" In addition to this, the farmer had to consider the resultant crop. Did a market exist for this product? Was it large enough to be profitable? Would the product be a designer commodity that captured consumer interest for a short period of time or would it stand the test of time? Did Elizabeth, a farmer, feel comfortable with the idea of working so closely with Coville, a scientist? Would their ideas mesh sufficiently to achieve success?

The negatives were addressed and either dismissed or resolved. As time went on, Frank Chambers would be able to assume some of the day-to-day cranberry tasks that consumed much of Elizabeth's time. "Huckleberries" had been an important food and medicine source since the days of the native peoples. Local Pineys enjoyed the treats from their favorite bushes, but a more urban population did not have the same opportunity unless they visited the area. Summer resorts were quite willing to pay a good price to be able to provide their guests with the tasty dessert.[47] As more of the population resided in cities, the consumer base for all agricultural products would grow. A major positive impetus for becoming part of the experiment was the idea that if they were involved from the beginning, and if the project was successful, the Whites would have learned the methodology and the pitfalls and would be poised to be a primary marketer of the new crop—at least for a time.

Elizabeth acknowledged that Coville "had a great deal of knowledge that could best be assimilated for use at Whitesbog if I had the opportunity to work with him."[48] More importantly, they would have been part of a historical and industry-changing contribution in the field of horticulture. This would not be her first collaboration with a scientist. In 1899–1900, Elizabeth had assisted Dr. Smith in finding a way to control the katydid infestation on her father's bogs. As she recounted to the cranberry growers, "The successful results of this investigation of Dr. Smith's . . . inspired a confidence in the possibility of scientific solutions of horticultural problems without which I never could have undertaken the blueberry work."[49] J. J. and Elizabeth had reached a decision. On January 11, 1911, Elizabeth penned the following letter to the United States Department of Agriculture.

B. T. Galloway, Chief. Bureau of Plant Industry, U. S. Dept. of Agriculture, Washington, D. C.

Dear Sir:

I recently received from Washington the report on "Experiments in Blueberry Culture," which I have read with great interest, and I write to make a suggestion in regard to future experiments.

My father, Joseph J. White, is one of the largest cranberry growers in the country, and on his property are considerable areas of land too high for cranberries but admirably suited to blueberries, judging by the way the wild ones flourish.

My father authorizes me to offer you the use of this land for further experiments in blueberry culture, and is willing to pay $50.00 a year for 5 years for such labor as may be needed in the experiments, we to have the proceeds from any crop that might be produced.

I should be pleased to assist in the work by observation, reports, or in any way in my power. If you should at all consider this proposition, Dr. Shear can perhaps give you some idea of our ability to assist the Dept. of Agriculture in this matter, as I had the pleasure of showing him and two of his assistants over a portion of our bogs last fall.

Trusting that this may receive favorable consideration, I am, Very respectfully yours,

Elizabeth C. White[50]

On the 25th anniversary of beginning blueberry experimentation at Whitesbog, Elizabeth recalled,

The carbon copy of that first letter written twenty-five years ago and the succeeding correspondence have been carefully preserved in a fire-proof safe. When the first letter was written I was sure it was of such importance in establishing a new branch of horticulture that the passage of time would give it historical value.[51]

By the end of January, the Whites received the reply they had desired. William Taylor, acting Chief of the Bureau, said that the department would probably accept their offer. Frederick Coville would have to be consulted. It did not take the scientist long to make up his mind. On February 4, Coville wrote saying he would like to visit Whitesbog to assess the possibilities. March 1, 1911, was set as the memorable date.[52] How Elizabeth must have prepared for and looked forward to that first meeting. Unfortunately, it was not to be. J. J. White had fallen seriously ill and had named his daughter as his surrogate in planning sessions regarding the newly formed Cranberry Cooperative. March 1 found Elizabeth negotiating to save the family's cranberry brand, White Star.

The Whites reached no formal agreement concerning blueberries with the USDA immediately; the signed contract came when the seedling plants were ready for field planting (1914). Much work needed to be completed prior to that point. The most immediate need was plant material for extended experimentation. Thus far, Coville's work involved primarily one source, the 'Brooks.' Elizabeth devoted the first five years of cooperation with Coville to the search for superior wild bushes. Anyone familiar with the blueberries growing in the vicinity of Whitesbog knew that innumerable individual characteristics made every blueberry plant distinct. In connection with the fruit, the important differences included size, color, flavor, texture, and time of ripening. The berries on one plant might be gone before those on another begin to ripen. For Joseph White and his daughter, only the best would do.

> Father and I often discussed the possibility of cultivating the swamp huckleberries but after spending hours sampling the fruit on bush after bush: finding the berries on one too sour for our taste, another too flat and insipid, a third plant too small to bother

with and so on for many plants and finding only an occasional bush on which the good sized berries had a most delicious flavor—'peachy' father called it—we decided that unless we could have only these best plants we did not want to have any.[53]

Elizabeth turned to the locals who sought the best blueberries in season to supplement their income. They, of all people, would know where the best specimens could be found, if they were willing to share their secrets. "I knew a good many people in our neighborhood, and they had known my father and grandfather if they didn't know me."[54] Miss Lizzie, as she was known to workers and neighbors, took a few of her trusted friends into her confidence, among them Alfred Stevenson and Ezekiel Sooy. That very summer, in July 1911, Ezekiel Sooy found three bushes just north of the road passing his home between Browns Mills and Whitesbog. They were called 'Sooy #1,' 'Sooy #2,' and 'Sooy #3.' On August 14, 1911, stem bases and budwood from 'Sooy #1' and 'Sooy #3' were sent to Washington, D.C., where Dr. Coville made extensive crosses with 'Brooks' and 'Sooy #1'[55] as the parents.

The marrying of these two bushes unearthed an important discovery. Individually, neither bush was viable commercial material. A number of the crosses, however, captured some of the good qualities of each, while minimizing some of the negatives. Cuttings from all three bushes were planted in Whitesbog. None made the grade as an independent variety and the bushes were discarded. In her log book, Elizabeth made a handwritten entry in November 1937, noting that three or four of 'Sooy #1' were kept in recognition of the part their finder had played in blueberry breeding.[56]

During the following summer, locals found other bushes, among them, the 'Rubel,' the 'Harding,' and the 'Chatsworth.' Elizabeth named each offering for its founder, using either the individual's first or last name. When it came to Rube Leek's bush, neither Elizabeth nor Coville could imagine naming "so noble" a bush either Rube or Leek. Dr. Coville suggested using the gentleman's full name but, at the time, the American Pomological Society had a single name standard for fruits. The botanist finally suggested taking the "L" from Leek and affixing it to "Rube." It was settled; the 'Rubel' was named.

The story of the 'Chatsworth' berry was quite different. Its berries were the largest Elizabeth had ever seen, measuring 3/4 inch; the fruit looked luscious. Elizabeth immediately notified Dr. Coville and treated it with the utmost care, thinking it was one of the best, if not the best, candidate they would find. Coville began to use it in his breeding. Elizabeth did not have a high opinion of its finder and since the gentleman died shortly after discovering the bush, she felt justified in breaking protocol by naming it after the location rather than the man. The 'Chatsworth' turned out to be a huge disappointment. The berries proved soft and mushy and had poor flavor. the plant also easily met with disease and proved of little value as a parent in breeding. To Elizabeth, the berry truly reflected its finder.[57]

The year 1913 proved a discouraging year for obtaining experimentation specimens. A heavy frost destroyed the entire crop of wild blueberries. The lull in full activity provided Elizabeth with time to organize her thoughts and to develop an actual collection strategy. She was ready when a large wild crop matured in 1914. Specimen jars had been prepared, outfitted with a formalin solution, labels, and a gauge to meet size requirements; fliers had been printed with directions for participating in the project and submitting entries, as well as payment schedules and amounts. Although, as previously noted, blueberries have many characteristics that would be considered in the selection process, size alone was included in White's instructions. Size would be definitive, as opposed to a subjective evaluation. Also, per the flier, White encouraged the woodsmen to carry the specimen set-ups with them so that they could take advantage of an unexpected find without making an extra trip. They also had the option of dropping the berries off at a central location. Elizabeth had no way to predict how long the berries had sat in the jars before she received them. In some instances, their quality had deteriorated significantly. A full evaluation of all characteristics would be obtained only after excavating the actual bushes during the resting season and cuttings taken.

In contrast to the previous year, 1914 saw the identification of many new bushes, among them the 'Adams,' 'Dunfee,'[58] and 'Grover.' The search continued for the ensuing two years, with the last wild bush, named the 'Sam,' for finder Sam Lemon, arriving at Whitesbog in 1916. Altogether, over the five years between 1911 and 1916, Elizabeth and crew moved 100 carefully selected New Jersey wild blueberry bushes to the trial fields at Whitesbog.

The locals collected blueberries and submitted them during the growing season, which lasted from late June until mid-August. The bush itself required rest, allowing the sap to return to the root system, before it could be dug up and moved. By the end of August, Elizabeth dedicated herself to the cranberry harvest, so she could not usually address this step in the process until late into October and November. Once again, she turned to the locals for assistance. As she told a reporter in 1951, "I never ceased to wonder how they led me through pathless thickets and undergrowth, where all the bushes looked alike to me, to the one bush which was producing berries superior to the surrounding plants in the bog."[59]

Elizabeth did not have the pleasure of bringing in Rube Leek's prize bush as she had suffered a major case of the grippe. Her brother-in-law, Frank Chambers, made sure that Whitesbog had safely received the bush. Thanksgiving Day, 1914, found Elizabeth deep in the woods around Chatsworth, instead of enjoying the holiday dinner with the family. Digging up and collecting bushes could be an arduous task. Some of the locations were accessible only by horseback. Recognizing this fact, Elizabeth was especially generous in compensating the woodsmen for leading her to the site and assisting her, paying them two or three times their normal daily wage. White once remarked that each bush brought to Whitesbog was treated as if it were the best bush ever and that it would prove to be the ultimate find. Cuttings were taken, sometimes as many as one hundred samplings.[60]

Once in place at the farm, Elizabeth dispatched a portion of each of the most promising bushes to

Dr. Coville, who used the materials as parents in his blueberry breeding. When large enough, Coville sent seedlings from his crosses back to Whitesbog for testing in the open field. In 1912, Coville crossed 'Brooks' and 'Sooy #1' to create 3,000 plants. One of these arrived in Whitesbog, known as 620-A; that is, the A bush of the 620th experimental culture of blueberry seeds or cuttings Dr. Coville made. The berry later received the name the 'Pioneer.' The following year, Coville once again crossed 'Sooy #1' with 'Brooks.'[61] He named the resulting cultivar 'Katharine,' in honor of his daughter. During field-testing, it carried the identifier of 830-C. Over the course of the years, 25,000 seedlings underwent testing at Whitesbog.[62] Of these, the USDA deemed only three hybrids acceptable for development—'Pioneer,' 'Katharine,' and 'Cabot.'

The formal contract between Joseph J. White, Inc., and the U.S. Department of Agriculture of 1914 provided for the government to pay $50 a year for four years as a rental fee for three acres of blueberry test fields. Each of the contracting parties had the right to half of the propagating material from any bush during the four-year test period. At the end of that period, the bushes and propagating material became the property of the Whites to do with as they pleased with one exception. They could not distribute propagating material from any bush without the express permission of the USDA. This agreement was renewed until 1928. The $50 fee was expected to cover the cost of supplies and labor. Supplemented by sales of berries and plant material, the funds proved sufficient at first. As more growers became involved, costs to Joseph J. White, Inc., became more prohibitive and the company withdrew from its collaboration with the USDA.

Between 1911 and 1916, all the blueberry work done was experimental but, finally, in 1916, a commercial crop, albeit small—only 17 crates—entered the marketplace.[63] Except for the small amount of berries the White family enjoyed, Whitesbog sold the entire crop to the Hudson River Day Line. This may seem a strange connection, but Abraham Hornor, chief purchaser for the Line, was brother to Ivens Hornor, Whitesbog's farm superintendent. Elizabeth's association with the Hornor family went back to her early childhood through her Grandfather Fenwick. With this sale, a new commercial agricultural industry commenced.

The White father and daughter set their sights on the future. Elizabeth had paid attention to J. J.'s advice to his fellow cranberry growers years before. If you are going to increase your product, make sure you pay attention to your consumer base. Advertise! In 1917, a rudimentary advertisement for blueberry plants went out in the form of a letter. The 'Rubel' was offered as the only "First Class" bush and the only bush guaranteed. Its price tag: a hefty $25.00. The others, still under testing, received classification as second and third class. The following year, the Whites prepared, printed, and distributed an actual catalog. It was the first of many, with each version becoming more sophisticated. A variety of cover letters accompanied the catalogs, each targeting a specific group of buyers: commercial growers, garden growers, even Massachusetts growers. Elizabeth didn't just say "Buy." She knew this was a virtually unknown commodity, so she shared her learned knowledge about blueberries.

J. J. White, Inc., provided information and hints in accompanying booklets, some giving general information on soil, moisture, and climate requirements; one addressing considerations for the Commercial Grower of Whitesbog Blueberries; still another directed to the Garden Grower. During a presentation made before the cranberry growers at their annual meeting on January 27, 1923, Elizabeth White announced a new, expanded, advertising approach. She says: "As of the first of the year [1923] we started a little experimental advertising, just a two inch insertion in *Country Gentleman* on January 6th and 20th and a quarter page in *The Garden Magazine*. As a result we already have received nearly 1900 inquiries from all over the United States and Canada."[64] Expanded advertising increased expenses but also improved sales, particularly of plants.[65] During this report on the progress of blueberry culture, White informed the assembly that five additional commercial blueberry plantations of Whitesbog Blueberries had been started in New Jersey.[66]

Experimentation did not stop once sales began; Elizabeth was an astute farmer and a thorough investigator. The success staring her in the face did not necessarily mean total success. To achieve that, she had to expand the test field. Around 1921, Joseph J. White, Inc., published a pamphlet called *An Experimental Farm in Miniature*. Cultivated blueberries grew splendidly in the Whitesbog vicinity of New Jersey, but would they do as well elsewhere? Elizabeth posed the question to the reader: which variety will grow best in your locality? We don't know now; we expect you to tell us so that as more plants become available for sale, we can recommend a particular variety for each locality. The brochure went on to describe the "Try and Report" Plan.

> Our "Try and Report" Plan calls for the delivery of one plant each of three of our choicest varieties for $3. Each set will include one plant each of Rubel and Harding, which we formerly sold for $25 each. This price does not cover the cost of the plants, nevertheless this isn't a "bargain offer," because these sets of three plants are sold only with the understanding that you report their progress from time to time. We particularly want to know how well these cultivated varieties succeed in other sections of the country. Only one set to a customer.[67]

There is no documentation to show if anyone participated in the trial or, if they did, the results. What it does show is the desire to provide every customer with the best product possible and the personal integrity of Elizabeth White as a business woman.

Elizabeth did not limit herself to sharing her blueberry knowledge through the printed word; she believed in a personal, hands-on touch. Her interaction with Louis Dammann, a fruit grower in Egg Harbor, New Jersey, was surely not an isolated occurrence. News of the blueberry experiment's success had trickled down to that area of South Jersey, as did the fact that the first sale had gone to New York. This did not set well with Louis, who wondered why Elizabeth had not chosen Atlantic City, a major resort center in her native New Jersey, as a profitable market for wild blueberries. Perhaps others wondered the same thing, since Uncle Daniel White owned the Traymore Hotel in that city. Did Louis express his disappointment to Elizabeth in a letter? It is unknown, but he did order 250 bushes, shipped to him in 1922. The contact between Elizabeth and Louis continued. Elizabeth paid Dammann a visit to assess his progress in becoming a commercial blueberry grower and to tutor him personally in all things blueberry.

When he took his first cultivated berries to the Atlantic City market in 1924, he received double the price over the market offering for wild berries, with no questions asked. Elizabeth must also have shown Dammann how to make cuttings from his bushes, for he was soon selling these to his fellow growers. This encounter may not seem like much, but when one takes distance and modes of transportation in the early 1920s into consideration, it represents a huge commitment of time and dedication.[68]

In addition to blueberry bushes, Joseph J. White, Inc., offered Franklinia trees, native pineland plants, and American holly for sale. This was an entirely new business venture for the corporation, and both J. J. and Elizabeth recognized the need for proper protocol and management. Sidney Hutton was brought in to identify and address the special requirements of this commercial offshoot (Hutton started in March 1919; he left in 1930). Arthur Morgan (of Antioch College fame) had recommended Hutton. How Elizabeth or her father knew Morgan is unknown, but they hired Hutton and it turned into a win-win situation for all concerned. The thoroughness with which he approached his duties is evident in an agenda he prepared for a meeting with the Whites, discussing plant sales, inventory, competition, soil and climate requirements, available markets, and advertising.[69]

Not many people recognize the name Sidney Hutton, but they do know his most memorable contribution to Whitesbog's blueberry enterprise. Shortly after his arrival, Hutton became aware of a unique packaging concept. He saw a box of Whitman Chocolates with a clear covering over the candies so the customer could see what he was purchasing. Sidney brought his idea to Elizabeth. Wouldn't blueberry sales increase if the buyer could see the lusciousness of the fruit? Up to that point, Whitesbog covered its quart boxes of blueberries with a simple paper wrapping. The Hudson River Day Line received its blueberries covered with plain brown paper squares which Elizabeth herself cut from large sheets and fastened with gummed paper. In 1917, Elizabeth replaced the squares with cut and imprinted manila covers which identified the contents as "Whitesbog Blueberries."[70]

While the name Whitesbog implied quality, Hutton reasoned that seeing was better than believing. He approached Whitman's management, who did not consider fruit to be a candy competitor. They provided Mr. Hutton with the name and location of the company that manufactured the clear material. What we call "cellophane" had not yet been brought to the United States and had to be imported from France. For the first time, shoppers could actually view the size and quality of the blueberries they were buying and were very happy about it! Sidney Hutton remained at Whitesbog until 1930, when he moved on to manage Conard-Pyle Star Roses in West Grove, Pennsylvania, another job Arthur Morgan negotiated. The Hutton Family still owns and operates this business.

As with any agricultural crop dependent on nature as well as the law of supply and demand, Whitesbog's blueberry sales fluctuated over the years.[71] Having competition from new blueberry growers also impacted sales to a degree. Below is a table of the size of saleable crop and the proceeds garnered each year from 1916 through 1927. Post-1927 sales occurred through the Tru-Blu Blueberry Cooperative. The steady increase in both crop size and receipts bode well for the new industry. Plant sales were not nearly so dramatic, which was to be expected, considering the potential customer base. In the table, annual receipts represent gross intake, not net profit. Production costs in the early years would have been significant. In fact, they provided the reason Joseph J. White, Inc., did not renew its testing lease agreement with the USDA in 1928.

The company accounting ledgers do not always record the sales of blueberry plants as distinct entries until 1921. From that date, they appear as aggregate dollar amounts by year. Between 1921 and 1927, inclusive, Whitesbog grossed $19,600 in receipts for the sale of all blueberry plants.

Whitesbog Blueberry Sales 1916 – 1927[72]

Year	Size of Crop Produced	Avg Price per Qt.	Annual Receipts
	Full crates – Quarts*		
1916	17	.22	$114.81
1917	96 – 18	.27	829.16
1918	100 – 5	.30	942.28
1919	309 – 3	.24	2,956.96
1920	533 – 24	.34	5,784.45
1921	309 – 24	.39	3,874.28
1922	966 – 14	.33	10,059.90
1923	712 – 19	.38	8,761.35
1924	761 – 4	.42	10,169.90
1925	1,121 – 1	.33	11,915.25
1926	924 – 13	.41	12,080.42
1927	2,280 – 1	.42	31,043.68

A full crate = 32 quarts

As more farmers joined the ranks of cultivated blueberry growers, Elizabeth White knew the time had arrived to take the next step. In 1927, she invited the local farmers already involved in blueberry culture to Suningive, her home at Whitesbog, and proposed that they form a Blueberry Cooperative. Most, if not all, also grew cranberries and had already been through the process with establishing the Cranberry Co-op.

Though a very painful experience, they had learned the pitfalls to be avoided and the problems to be faced. Elizabeth probably knew the difficulties better than anyone, having been so intimately associated with J. J. as he tried to steer the American Cranberry Exchange (later EATMOR) into being. She would not have her father to guide her through this new endeavor since he died three years before.

The organizational activity quickly moved forward. On June 22, 1927, the Blueberry Cooperative Association, later to be known as Tru-Blu, was established. Joseph J. White, Inc., was Grower #1. According to the by-laws, each member, whether individual or corporation, was entitled to only one vote so that larger growers could not control or dominate smaller farmers when creating policy. Also, to be a member, one had to be a grower. Elizabeth White, the prime mover of the entire industry, did not qualify. After J. J. White's death, Frank Chambers became the elected president of Joseph J. White, Inc., and it was he who represented and voted for the Corporation.

Once again, Sidney Hutton played a central role. He and Elizabeth founded the Hutton-White Blueberry Farm at Rake Pond, on a plot of land that was part of J. J.'s holdings. Their company became Grower #10, with Elizabeth White as representative. In addition, Hutton had a private farm in Pemberton and became Grower #8. Even though Sidney Hutton moved on to Conard-Pyle and Star Roses, the Hutton-White farm continued to be maintained until Elizabeth's stroke in 1945, when the company formally dissolved. After that time, she no longer had eligibility for membership, but the other members would not let such a travesty happen. In 1946, by unanimous vote, Elizabeth White received an honorary lifetime membership.

Her affiliation with the blueberry growing community had changed, but Elizabeth was no stranger to changing relationships in her life. One of the most significant had been her association with Frederick Coville. Elizabeth described it as "the beginning of a period of cooperative experimentation of intense interest and remarkable results."[73]

This may sound like satisfaction with the successful outcome of an intellectual pursuit, but it was much more than that. Both parties had completely immersed themselves in the project, emotionally and spiritually, as well as intellectually. Elizabeth's own recollection confirms this assertion. "Those first blueberry years are a joyous memory. Encouraging developments came thick and fast. Dr. Coville and I gloated over them together, the enthusiasm of each fanning to brighter flame that of the other."[74] How did Coville feel about their venture together? *The Newark Evening News* quoted his commendation of Elizabeth. "Miss White, by her experiments at Whitesbog, has advanced the culture of blueberries at least fifty years over what it otherwise would have been."[75]

As the old adage says, "All good things must come to an end." For White and Coville the separation was triggered, as so many life transitions, by circumstances beyond their control. In this case, it was the passing of Joseph J. White in May 1924. On the 25th anniversary of the blueberry experiment, Elizabeth reminisced,

> This cooperation closed when the new responsibilities falling on me after my father's death and the growing claims of blueberries as a commercial crop made it impossible for me to give the close personal attention to co-operative experiments, which characterized the earlier years of work.[76]

This closure did not in any way signify the end of White's work with blueberries, as seen in the formation of Tru-Blu. She began her own hybridization experiments in 1928, using the methods she had learned from Dr. Coville. J. Harold Clark, reporting for the New Jersey Horticultural Society, noted that, by 1946, Elizabeth had raised hundreds of thousands of blueberry seedlings. He also observed that the rigorous quality controls she imposed resulted in relatively few plants making it to numbered row testing in the field.

Throughout her life, Elizabeth White was a reflective and spiritual person. She pondered the meaning of events and actions. Sometimes she shared her thoughts with others; sometimes the sharing was at an unlikely time or event. In January 1917, Elizabeth delivered an address to the Daughters of the American Revolution in Camden on the subject of "The Pineys of New Jersey." Toward the end of this talk, she explains her understanding of the entire blueberry project, its place in history, and the expanse of collaboration required to achieve the progress made to that point and to be hoped for in the future.

> I think that now days God is making many revelations of his truth through the scientific workers,

and through the practical workers too, who are fitting the bits of truth discovered by the scientists into the everyday scheme of life. It is somewhat like working out an elaborate picture puzzle. The whole is perfectly planned but there are only disconnected parts of it that mankind has been enabled to piece together so as here and there to get an imperfect idea of the design. The scientists are searching for the missing pieces, and with the practical workers are trying to fit them to the parts that already seem finished. Sometimes a new bit will be discovered which obviously requires the rearrangement of quite a section which had seemed properly fitted together, and when the rearrangement is accomplished it is seen that very considerable progress has been made in working out the picture.

Every business and vocation has its place in this great puzzle picture . . . The last few years my attention has been especially held by the little corner of the puzzle where the blueberries fit in. No one had paid much attention to this corner till a scientist at Washington about ten years ago began to hunt for bits that belonged there. He found a number of pieces that fitted together so nicely he felt sure the group was a part of the great picture and published a bulletin about them.

When father and I read the bulletin we believed that the group of blueberry bits would just fit into the group of cranberry bits on which we had been working, and tried it there. So far it seems to fit perfectly. Then we saw that the pineys had a piece that belonged with the others. Their knowledge of the woods and swamps enabled them to locate the exceptionally fine wild blueberry plants which bear berries of a size and quality

surpassing anything we dreamed of six years ago, . . .
essential to the perfection of the whole.[77]

Elizabeth White's contributions to blueberry culture
were not soon forgotten. In 1966, twelve years after
her death, the New Jersey Blueberry Council selected
a cultivar that had large, sweet berries of medium blue
and named it 'Elizabeth' in her honor. Elizabeth had
cultivated this blueberry and grown it successfully at
Whitesbog for several years as 3850-A. The 'Elizabeth'
blueberry is known for its intense rich flavor, making
it a favorite of chefs because of its high dessert quality.
It is not usually grown commercially, however, since
it is not as hardy as originally thought, and does not
ship well.

Holly Haven

In 1950, Elizabeth White took a huge step; she moved her blueberry, holly, and native plant nursery from Whitesbog to Upton, a new venue just a short distance away along today's Route 70. She was just weeks away from her 79th birthday, rather late in life to embark on so challenging a venture. The reason behind her decision is not documented anywhere, but it was probably rooted in occurrences at Whitesbog at the time.

Money invested in the Whitesbog Conservation Nursery declined steadily through the 1940s, as the company concentrated its focus on improving commercial crop production. Additionally, the demand for blueberry bushes had declined. The Whitesbog nursery began supplying growers with plants in 1918 and provided the pioneering commercial market well. The Blueberry Cooperative, as well as other nurseries, then offered plants to newcomers and expanders. Logic dictated the need to reduce plant propagation and concentrate on commercial production.

Another reason to phase out plant production might stem from the fact that Elizabeth no longer had Tom Windon working as her propagator. Elizabeth hired Thomas Windon in 1923 as the primary blueberry propagationist. Windon had earned a degree in horticulture from the University of Massachusetts. After graduation, the USDA hired him to assist in the experimental work on cultivated blueberries.[78] In addition to his employment at Whitesbog, Windon had his own personal blueberry farm. In 1941, the United States government evicted several blueberry farmers to accommodate the expansion of Fort Dix, Thomas Windon among them. He made the decision to move his family to Maryland, where he started a new blueberry farm.

Concomitant with Windon's departure, Joseph J. White, Inc., began experiencing internal problems. From correspondence between Elizabeth and leaders of the two cranberry marketing organizations competing for control, it becomes quite clear that disagreement and friction had arisen between her and the other directors of Joseph J. White, Inc., with respect to the direction the company should take. Additionally, when Frank Chambers, long-time President of Joseph J. White, Inc., died in 1947, Joseph Darlington, the eldest son of Beulah White Darlington, succeeded Chambers.[79] Joe had begun working at Whitesbog in the mid-1930s. He quickly adjusted to his new responsibilities as president and began making his mark in the cranberry community when he tragically died in an airplane crash on August 14, 1948. For a time, the fate of Whitesbog hung in the balance; continuity as a family-run operation was questionable.

Only two family members were young enough to be considered viable leaders of Joseph J. White, Inc.: Elizabeth Chambers, daughter of Frank and Anne White Chambers, and Thomas Darlington, Joe's younger brother and son of Lewis and Beulah White Darlington. Miss Chambers resided in Europe, and Thomas was just getting established in a satisfying and what looked like a very successful engineering career with Westinghouse. The corporation remained without a head for almost two years. Without a successor, the possibility existed that Whitesbog might be sold. However, Elizabeth was not yet ready to give up her life's work; it is doubtful that her lexicon included the word "retirement." Possessing a business acumen formed from her father, Elizabeth would have begun to prepare for an eventual sale of the farm.

For any one of the above reasons, or for all of them taken together, Elizabeth decided the time had come to strike out on her own. By the time she was ready to take a definitive step toward accomplishing her goal, Tom Darlington had agreed to relinquish his own plans and to assume management of Joseph J. White, Inc. Whitesbog would continue and thrive, but Elizabeth decided to follow through with her independent enterprise, which she called Holly Haven. According to the recorded deed of Burlington County, Elizabeth C. White, June Vail, and Jacob Homer[80] bought a six-acre tract of land from Abram and Bessie Brown on July 28, 1950. Work began immediately to set up the new site. In August, following a meeting with Tom Darlington, Harold Haines, and Bert Jarvis, Mr. Homer, as agreed, received notification in writing from Joseph J. White, Inc., requiring him to remove equipment and plant materials from the Whitesbog nursery. Deadlines of June, July, and December 1951 were set forth for various activities. Two points in the memorandum are of special interest. One states that Joseph J. White, Inc., will give Homer the sash house (a simple glass house) now in use, including the complete heating system. The second is that the new nursery will be able to take cuttings of hollies left at Whitesbog.[81] No mention was made of blueberries and, in 1952, Elizabeth's attempt to secure blueberry samples led to a rather nasty confrontation with Tom Darlington, which the USDA settled in her favor. Homer's direct negotiations with Joseph J. White, Inc., and the resultant wording used in the memo, seems to imply that Jacob Homer was familiar with the Whitesbog nursery operation. Could he have been a replacement for Tom Windon?

Elizabeth, and others, brought Jack Cadbury and Mark Cutts onboard; Holly Haven began to take shape. In addition to the sash house from Whitesbog, three more were constructed, along with two greenhouses, some potting sheds, and a pump house. Crews prepared fields and planted blueberry plants, hollies, and Franklinia. Almost a year later, on May 24, 1951, the partners officially transferred the property to Holly Haven, Inc., a New Jersey corporation based at Whitesbog with the following officers: Elizabeth White, President; J. Homer, Vice-president; and June Vail, Secretary.

Rudimentary advertising the first year consisted of simple mimeographed lists featuring only holly. From its very name, this first catalog, and later, from more professional advertising pamphlets, Elizabeth made it clear that holly would be the star of her new venture. One catalog has a personal introduction of Holly Haven's president on the first page. It describes Elizabeth as having "turned her experienced eye to the selection of the best native holly, *Ilex opaca*."[82]

Elizabeth invited the public to take advantage of her years of searching and experimenting. "Now you can have, at modest cost, the choicest of American Hollies, proven by time, chosen personally by Miss White, a holly expert."[83] The many offerings listed varied, including some of Wilfrid Wheeler's selections like 'Amy' and 'St. Mary,' as well as Earle Dilatush's favorite, 'Old Heavy Berry.' One of Holly Haven's advertising brochures listed hollies by gender, noting females have red berries (as opposed to yellow); and each named offering was accompanied with a description and an illustration of the leaf. Available male pollinators followed with their descriptions and leaf drawings.

American holly was not the sole product of Holly Haven nursery. Select species producing black berries, like *Ilex glabra* (inkberry), also found their way into the mix for those seeking evergreen shrubs. The nursery's offerings included six named blueberry cultivars, but the catalog also noted the availability of other bushes. Orders for blueberries were by quantity only. Depending on the number of plants ordered, the nusery shipped from five to ten varieties. Franklinia and bearberry also found their way onto the menu. Inventory was constantly being replenished. In 1953, June Vail notes that 64,000 holly cuttings were taken and planted, comprising 47,000 female and 17,000 male.

Holly Haven was still in its start-up phase when Elizabeth died on November 27, 1954. Desiring to "make it a profitable venture for the officers and workers and a contribution to the general welfare of the neighborhood," she left instructions in her Last Will and Testament that her "common stock is to be distributed among directors and workers at Holly Haven, Inc., in such a proportion as will best strengthen the organization."[84] The nursery continued to operate actively for six more years before the corporation's dissolution on December 13, 1960. Upon dissolving, Jack Cadbury III took possession of the nursery and its operations.

Elizabeth's holly initiatives were celebrated not only in her lifetime, but also after her death. Her good friend, Wilfrid Wheeler, along with William Makepeace, honored her by selecting a special tree which they named 'Elizabeth.' The two friends dug up the special tree and removed it to Ashumet Farm. C. R. Wolf followed suit, naming his tribute 'Miss White.' Holly Haven introduced the latter tree in 1956.[85]

June Vail

It is impossible to talk about Elizabeth White, her garden, the Whitesbog nursery, and Holly Haven, without mentioning June Vail, Elizabeth's assistant, companion, and friend. June came to Whitesbog in 1945 at age 24. After high school, she attended a two-year course in horticulture at what was then the Pennsylvania School of Horticulture for Women in Ambler, Pennsylvania, now part of Temple University. The following three years (1942–1945) Vail spent in plant propagation at Ambler Nurseries.

Before June's arrival, Elizabeth had a secretary who left to be married. Since this first young woman had attended Ambler, Elizabeth thought that she should consult the same place for a replacement. The potential successors included June Vail. After a brief interview with Elizabeth and a tour of Whitesbog, June received an offer for the position. She was the perfect candidate, having grown up in Pennsylvania on a farm with greenhouses where she learned about plant propagation and having taken the landscaping course at Ambler.

Elizabeth and June "clicked" from the beginning. In a 2008 interview, June recalled, "When I arrived at Whitesbog for the interview, I knew right away this is what I wanted to do. It was like a dream come true."[86] It did not take her long to move into Suningive. June worked in the greenhouses and outside. Before 8 a.m., she tended Elizabeth's garden at Suningive, pulling weeds and adding new plants like pink lady slipper or orange milkwort. From 9 a.m. to 4 p.m., June worked with blueberry, holly, bearberry, and other native plant cuttings both at Whitesbog and later at Holly Haven. In addition to her assigned tasks, June found time to create a vegetable garden, from which she contributed to the household larder.

June Vail was, most of all, a true friend to Elizabeth. She had been at Whitesbog for about six months when Elizabeth had a stroke that affected her speech and mobility. She suffered partial paralysis for six months, fighting all the while to recover the full use of her faculties. Although there were homemakers and nurses brought in specifically to deal with Elizabeth's incapacitation, it was June who helped her the most during the difficult process of rehabilitation. She moved her bedroom from the second to the third floor to be close to Elizabeth's room. She learned to drive Elizabeth's car so she could take her to doctor visits. She kept up the nursery work and maintained Elizabeth's beloved garden. When White could not travel, she sent June Vail to visit Wilfrid Wheeler for holly hunting and selecting. Wheeler's reaction to June was that he and his wife loved her and wanted to keep her. Of course, they returned her to her beloved "Miss White." When Elizabeth succumbed to cancer nine years later, it was June Vail who sat and held her hand as she passed into the next life. However, before this sad event occurred, there was so much life to be lived and so many things to be accomplished.

After her departure from Whitesbog and Holly Haven, June remained in the field of horticulture. From 1957 to 1964, she worked for Burpee Seed Company in the Customer Service Department, answering questions and giving lectures to garden clubs, among other duties. On August 1, 1964, June joined the staff of the Pennsylvania Horticultural Society before moving on to become head gardener at Pennsbury Manor, William Penn's reconstructed summer home in Bucks County, Pennsylvania. She finally retired to her family's cottage in the Poconos, where she remained until her death on November 27, 2012. June's love for and loyalty to Miss White endured to the end and was immediately evident to anyone who spoke with her. When still physically able, June gave talks about Elizabeth to members of the Pennsylvania Horticultural Society and attendees at the Pinelands Short Course, among others.

Franklinia

A singular gem in Elizabeth White's nursery was the Franklin tree. Tradition has it that Frederick Coville introduced her to it. Exotic in name (*Franklinia alatamaha*) and mysterious in history, the Franklinia has evoked interest and botanical research since John and William Bartram first discovered the plant more than two centuries ago. John Bartram, a Quaker farmer, was fascinated with plants of every kind, sufficiently enough that he taught himself Latin so that he could learn the plant classification system. In 1728, he purchased land along the Schuylkill River in Philadelphia and established Bartram's Garden, the first botanical garden in the United States, existing to the present day.

Bartram gained fame as a botanist both in America and Europe. William Bartram, the third son, inherited his father's deep affection for nature. In 1765, John traveled to North Carolina, where William was living at the time, and the two went on a botanic exploration of Georgia and eastern Florida. While near Fort Barrington along the banks of the Altamaha River in Georgia, father and son came upon a cluster of trees they had never seen before. John Bartram recounts in his journal for October 1, 1765, "This day we found several very curious shrubs, one bearing beautiful good fruite."[87]

There is no record that, at this first encounter, they collected either plants or seeds to bring home. William describes the tree in his *Travels*.

> In the course of these excursions and researches, I had the opportunity of observing the new flowering shrub, resembling the Gordonia in perfect bloom, as well as bearing ripe fruit. It is a flowering tree, of the first order for beauty and fragrance of blossoms: the tree grows fifteen or twenty feet high, branching alternately; the leaves are oblong, broadest towards their extremities, and terminate with an acute point, which is generally a little reflexed; they are lightly serrated, attenuate downwards and sessile, or have very short petioles; they are placed in alternate order, and towards the extremities of the twigs are crouded together, but stand more sparsedly below; the flowers are very large, expand themselves perfectly, are of a snow-white colour, and ornamented with a crown or tassel of gold coloured refulgent staminae in their centre; the inferior petal or segment of the corolla is hollow, formed like a cap or helmet, and entirely includes the other four, until the moment of expansion; its exterior surface is covered with a short silky hair; the borders of the petals are crisped or plicated: these large, white flowers stand single and sessile in the bosom of the leaves, which being near together towards the extremities of the twigs, and usually many expanded at the same time, make a gay appearance; the fruit is a large, round, dry, woody apple or pericarpe, opening at each end oppositely by five alternate fissures, containing ten cells, each replete with dry

woody cuniform seed. This very curious tree was first taken notice of, about ten or twelve years ago, at this place, when I attended my father (John Bartram) on a botanical excursion; but, it being then late in the autumn, we could form no opinion to what class or tribe it belonged.

We never saw it grow in any other place, nor have I ever since seen it growing wild, in all my travels, from Pennsylvania to Point Coupe, on the banks of the Mississippi, which must be allowed a very singular and unaccountable circumstance; at this place there are two or three acres of ground where it grows plentifully.

On first observing the fructification and habit of this tree, I was inclined to believe it a species of Gordonia, but afterwards, upon stricter examination, and comparing its flowers and fruit with those of the *Gordonia lasianthus*, I presently found striking characteristics abundantly sufficient to separate it from that genus, and to establish it the head of a new tribe, which we have honoured with the name of the illustrious Dr. Benjamin Franklin, *Franklinia Alatamaha.*[88]

Moses Marshall, son of botanist Humphry Marshall,[89] located the grove near Fort Barrington in 1790, while on a collecting expedition. This was the last confirmed sighting of *Franklinia* in the wild. The disappearance of *Franklinia alatamaha* from Georgia has long been a mystery. Several theories have been put forth, from destruction by man of the trees or their habitat or, possibly, to their succumbing to diseases because of a lack of genetic diversity. It has also been suggested that the Franklinia originally grew in more northern climes and "moved" south during the ice age. When the ice sheet melted, it could not survive in the hotter climate. While the theories are interesting and thought-provoking, it is dubious that botanists will ever definitively identify the reason for Franklinia's disappearance. Despite his being characterized as having affection for his subjects, Bartram's description of the Franklinia tree and flower is factual, almost mundane; quite appropriate for a botanist. Elizabeth had the freedom to present this gem to the public with poetic eloquence.

> Franklin's tree is rarely beautiful in detail and marvelous in its landscape effect. Moreover, it blooms at a season when few shrubs or trees are in flower.
>
> The slender trunk and graceful flowers are so muscular and sinewy in appearance that one almost expects motion, as under a greyhound's satin skin. Its smooth, dark grey bark has markings of lighter color wavering lengthwise.
>
> Each twig develops at its tip a cluster of buds of graduated size, like overgrown greenish pearls, and the largest of these attain the size of marbles by early August. The guard petal then falls back, but the bud still retains its spherical form. From its shelter then emerge four other petals, satiny, snowy white, elaborately frilled and pleated. The snowy chalice, 3 inches in diameter, holds a mass of orange-gold stamens, and breathes a delicate, balmy fragrance. Each flower lasts two to three days and then drops cleanly, There is a constant succession of bloom till hard frost.[90]

The Franklinia was a staple in the Whitesbog nursery from the beginning, and, later, at Holly Haven. It is logical that the city of Philadelphia would have an affinity for the Franklinia. When the Franklin Institute moved to its newly constructed quarters, circa 1933, the architects incorporated three Whitesbog-grown *Franklinia alatamaha* into the landscape. Elizabeth White received an invitation to the ceremonial planting and looked on proudly as Charles F. Jenkins did the honors. Mr. Jenkins was a prominent Quaker historian and horticulturist. In addition to being a member, he served as President of the Historical Society of Pennsylvania. Concomitantly with the Franklinia planting, Jenkins became involved in another project in which Elizabeth also participated—Penn Trees.

Elizabeth's Nurseries

When Whitesbog's nursery began, it focused on providing blueberry plants for commercial sales, and it retained that focus until around 1940. As much as Elizabeth wanted to share her blueberry experience with others, she also desired to provide them with the delights she found in the beauty of pineland flora. She sold some of the best the area had to offer like pine barren gentian, swamp magnolia, sand myrtle, trailing arbutus, bearberry, and, of course, holly. Although not pineland natives, Elizabeth included white and purple heather and Franklinia in her offerings. Given the economic impetus to share in the profits of commercial blueberry growing, it is no surprise that blueberry cuttings and plants were the biggest sellers. As late as 1939, the financial ledgers posted sales of 41,000 blueberry cuttings and 9,000 plants 10" – 12". Franklinia placed second, at least during the 1930s, the only decade that differentiated sales in the accounting records. Sales in 1937 proved to be the best for Franklin's tree, totaling 2100 sold. Sales during 1940 came in not far behind with 1833 trees sold. The other years comprising the decade averaged 700 to 800 trees purchased from the nursery.

Holly sales numbers were a distant third to blueberry and Franklinia. Most years saw 300 trees of varying sizes sold, but 1938 broke the trend with 704 purchase slips. Given the public's hesitancy to become involved with holly—many thought the plants difficult to transplant and arrange and suspected its suitability for the New Jersey climate—these numbers are not surprising. Elizabeth used her intriguing writing ability to induce potential holly buyers through an appeal to New Jersey Garden Clubs. She attempted to reduce their reluctance by providing the "how-to," just as she had done for potential blueberry growers. She also suggested that home holly gardens could be a source of income by furnishing holly branches for Christmas decorating.

While the overall numbers may seem substantial in terms of plant matter sold, the average yearly gross proceeds generated from all retail sales were approximately $2,500, with some more prosperous years seeing double this amount. Prices, which were standard for this era, ranged from $0.01 for blueberry cuttings sold and $0.25 for small blueberry plants to $4.00 for 4-foot Franklinia trees. Whitesbog's nursery also supplied the Blueberry Cooperative with plants to sell to members and, for this service, shared in a percentage of the profits. Sales comprised only half of the equation. One cannot lose sight of the fact that many expenditures associated with producing inventory and generating sales such as advertising, coal for greenhouse heating, postage, transportation, fertilizer, and, of course, human labor, filled out the other half of the equation. It is difficult to quantify actual income generated from the nursery since numerous blueberry plants produced were planted right at Whitesbog in the commercial blueberry fields. Such usage contributed to nursery expenses, but not to the sales.

Reflection on the breadth of planning required to carry on her blueberry experimentation, and to establish the nursery, leads one to conclude that Elizabeth White was an extremely logical and organized person. Before she decided to start Holly Haven, she likely considered all aspects of such an undertaking. First and foremost, a business had to have the potential to generate a return on investment. Twenty-five plus years of experience and financial records afforded more than enough data for analysis. Elizabeth would have to justify making holly the primary product offering; it had never been a big seller at Whitesbog. By the end of the 1940s, however, the horticultural landscape began to change. Just as the country had awakened to the world of blueberries, interest in holly soon flourished, particularly with the formation of the Holly Society of America.

Being her father's daughter, Elizabeth was willing to take the calculated risk. Most of all, she had to be true to her passionate need to experiment and to conserve. If there was one business lesson that J. J. White taught his daughters and employees, and which Elizabeth mastered, it was that quality mattered both in the product and how it was delivered. Aside from the underlying Quaker ethic of honesty, he knew that a satisfied customer would be a repeat customer. White's cranberries were highly sought by merchants; Elizabeth constantly tried to improve blueberries to meet the needs of growers and the marketplace. This same mindset carried over to the nursery operation.

A guarantee of satisfaction accompanied every plant or tree sold, whether the customer carted it or the nursery shipped it.

> Our guarantee is the Golden Rule of honest people. We guarantee them true to name and to arrive in good condition. Notify us immediately if shipment arrives damaged.[91]

The many letters from pleased buyers demonstrate that Joseph J. White, Inc., kept its promise. Elizabeth's clientele knew that she, not the site, was the source of the quality and that, therefore, they could expect the same treatment from Holly Haven.

With the financial analysis completed, committed investors provided the necessary start-up funds. The basic equipment was available and a sufficient inventory of holly already existed, along with an enthusiastic labor force, ready to join the project. Hence, Elizabeth White's new nursery came into being.

Elizabeth C. White the Social Advocate: NCLC (National Child Labor Committee)

The 1910 Whitesbog cranberry harvest began on September 3. Ivins Hornor, White's farm superintendent, predicted 48,000 bushels. By the beginning of August, all indications were that it would be even more plentiful and would require more than the usual allotment of pickers, most of whom were Italian immigrants recruited from South Philadelphia. Whitesbog had been supplementing the neighborhood work force with Italians for several years already.

During the mid-nineteenth century, a good many residents, not engaged full time on cranberry plantations, also worked at Hanover Furnace or Mary Ann Forge in the bog iron industry. Richard and Samuel Jones had purchased Hanover Furnace and Mary Ann Forge from their father, Benjamin Jones, in 1846. The brothers recognized the impending demise of the iron industry in southern New Jersey; iron ore was both more easily accessible and more affordable in nearby Pennsylvania. In 1857, Richard Jones opened the Florence Iron Works along the banks of the Delaware River. Many Pine Barrens residents, together with their families, followed Jones to his new factory in Florence, New Jersey, causing cranberry growers to lose employees.

When Hanover Furnace closed around 1864, the pool of local cranberry pickers diminished even more. An alternate labor source had to be found for cranberry harvesting, particularly after 1882, when J. J. White took over management of the Fenwick property and began to add his own bogs. Two historic movements converged to answer the need. The Unification of Italy led to many dissatisfied citizens leaving Southern Italy for the United States. At the same time, the Industrial Revolution brought a major shift in occupations, especially in the northeast states in America. As people moved into urban centers and obtained manufacturing employment, the need for a ready food supply grew, while the pool of agricultural workers to harvest the crops shrank. For Philadelphia's population, South Jersey farmers were more than willing to supply the first need and the city's Italian immigrants, the second. For the Italian women, the New Jersey crop harvests took place when a hiatus occurred in the city's garment and hat trades in which many found employment. According to historian Cindy Hahamovitch, it was essential that they look for interim opportunities since "it was the labor of married women and children that made the difference between subsistence and starvation."[92]

Ivins Hornor's predictions proved correct for the 1910 harvest. By September 20, the Whites had shipped 40,000 bushels of Early Blacks[93] and, when the picking was completed on October 15, the year's harvest had reached a record 54,400 bushels, the largest crop ever.

Others maintained an interest in the New Jersey cranberry harvest that year, but they were neither cranberry growers nor farm laborers. Elizabeth sets the stage for a dilemma with which she would struggle for the next thirty-plus years.

> During the fall of 1910 a Mr. Brown spent a week or more at Pemberton, N.J., visiting the bogs within easy reach, ours among them. He represented a magazine syndicate, he said, and expressing himself much pleased with his interview promised to send me a copy of any article resulting from his visit to the bog.
>
> He and a companion, who sometimes accompanied him, took many photographs and left our Italian bosses with the impression that they were to receive copies of the pictures. The whole body of pickers was on the *qui vive* to see those pictures and for the remainder of the season I was unable to answer the numerous questions showered upon me in regard to them.[94]

Mr. Edward Brown and his companion, Mr. Lewis Hine, did not represent a magazine syndicate. They were investigators for the National Child Labor Committee,[95] sent to expose alleged abuses by the cranberry growers toward the migrant workers, particularly the children. Agriculture was the current focus of interest for the committee in what had been and would continue to be a systematic disclosure of child exploitation by American industry.

Elizabeth did not receive a copy of the promised magazine article; the pickers saw no pictures for which many of them had so proudly posed. Instead, just before Thanksgiving 1910, the public at large was greeted with NCLC published Leaflet No. 34, displaying the hardships imposed on the youngest and weakest cranberry pickers by unfeeling farm owners and requesting funds to continue the fight against such blatant injustice. Joseph White, his family, and his fellow growers were oblivious to the fact that they were in the eye of an oncoming storm.

This was not the first time the cranberry growers had been targeted for using children to pick their berries. In 1905, the Philadelphia and New Jersey Consumer Leagues hired an investigative reporter named Mina C. Ginger to research children at work in the fields (all farm fields, not just cranberry bogs). Absence from school became the focus of concern for these agencies. The exodus, which left the lower grades of both public and parochial schools in Philadelphia almost depopulated, began in late April or early May, when families took off to participate in New Jersey's strawberry season. When this crop had finished, they moved on to picking raspberries and blackberries. By the time the small berry season concluded, tomatoes had ripened and were ready for picking. The hired hands thus picked their way through the summer season.

Some families migrated from crop to crop; some were more selective and participated in only one or two harvests. Some stopped when school reopened in September, but many families chose to take part in one final harvest: the cranberry harvest. Children who accompanied their parents to both the early and late fruit picking crops lost between three and four months of schooling. This extended period served as the crux of the controversy.

Mina Ginger published her findings in the January 1907 issue of *The Trainman's Journal* in an article entitled, "In Berry Field and Bog." The cranberry growers seemed to be as unaware of this earlier study[96] as they were of the NCLC publication. Just as Mr. Brown did not send Elizabeth White that promised copy (perhaps because Leaflet No. 34 was not a magazine article), so too, it is unlikely that anyone from *The Trainman's Journal* or either of the two Consumer Leagues sent a copy of Ginger's article to any of the berry growers. There was a decided difference, however, in the effect of the two reports.

The influence of either Consumer League, Pennsylvania or New Jersey, which had sponsored Ginger's investigation, was undoubtedly local and minimal at best. The National Child Labor Committee, on the other hand, was, as its name implied, national in its membership and extensive in its influence, especially due to some of its members like former president Grover Cleveland, Harvard President Charles Eliot, and Jane Addams of Chicago's Hull House. Fortunately, J. J. White had a friend who sent him one of the NCLC leaflets. Now the cranberry growers, particularly in New Jersey, knew what the NCLC wrote, or, more accurately, knew about the fight that lay ahead. Most of them probably could not envision the multi-faceted scrutiny that would be imposed on the industry or the time and energy that would be devoted to defending themselves, but Joseph J. White could.

J. J. White was a man of action. We do not know who forwarded him the leaflet (Elizabeth remarks only that it was a friend),[97] but as soon as he received and digested it, he penned a response to the Committee on behalf of himself and his fellow growers. On November 29, 1910, White sent an introductory letter to National Child Labor Committee, Inc., describing some of the statements as sensational and misleading, and others as complete falsehoods. Owen R. Lovejoy, General Secretary of the Committee, responded immediately. Lovejoy assured White that the Committee was dedicated to accuracy and would appreciate knowing which of its statements constituted falsehoods. The primary accusations leveled against the growers included forced child labor, substandard living conditions, and an unhealthful, disagreeable environment. Once again, addressing the entire Committee, J. J. White refuted specific charges, taking four, single-spaced, typewritten pages to do so. In a handwritten note at the end of the copy he kept, J. J. indicated that he had sent copies of the letter to Felix Adler, Chairman of the Board of Trustees, and to members Jane Addams and Edward T. Devine.[98] Again, Owen Lovejoy wrote back, defending the Committee's stance. Mr. White had one final communication with the General Secretary, addressing the letter specifically to him. The final sentence probably best conveys the mood of the entire community of cranberry growers.

> If you really had the welfare of the children at heart, do you not think it would have been better, and more honorable, to have first called the attention of the growers to their own delinquencies, instead of saying nothing to them, but saying ugly things to others about them?[99]

Lovejoy's rejoinder on January 13, 1911, was a list of suggestions for improvements that White and the other growers should take under advisement. By the time J. J. received this missive, he was too ill to answer. He left the conflict in the capable hands of his daughter and confidante, Elizabeth.[100]

One week prior to the January 13 letter, even after hearing from and responding to J. J. White, Owen Lovejoy published an extensive article in the *Survey* entitled, "The Cost of The Cranberry Sauce," that fleshed out the accusations which had appeared in the original pamphlet. He even referenced White's comments. Once again, the growers received no notification of Lovejoy's article. This time, J. J. received a copy from his labor recruiter, Gus Donato, who, in turn, had obtained it from a little girl who picked berries with her family at Whitesbog. The child saw the magazine lying on a table at Madonna House[101] and, recognizing the girl on the cover as a fellow picker at Whitesbog, excitedly reported what she had seen. Donato scoured the newsstands, but could not find a single copy of that issue of *Survey*. He asked for and received the copy at Madonna House. The title of Lovejoy's article is significant. Association of working conditions and a consumer product was aimed at hitting the industry at the economic level. Loss of sales might accomplish what words would not.

Through the years, certain individuals supported the cranberry growers; Mr. Robert C. Sanger was one such person. These supporters read or listened to accusations discerningly, attempting to sift fact from fiction. After reading Lovejoy's January 7, 1911, article, Sanger wrote a letter to the editor questioning some facts.[102] Lovejoy's response is telling. He admits to seeing nothing first hand. Instead, he relied on the report of two agents and, being under pressure to have the article ready for print, had asked someone else to fact check for him. We cannot fault any member of the NCLC for their motivation in addressing what was the actual abuse of children in many industries in the United States. Rather, sweeping generalities were the triggers that opened a Pandora's Box. It would take many decades to overcome the distrust and ill-will let loose by a simple leaflet designed to encourage compassion and generosity.

Although Elizabeth would eventually confront Owen Lovejoy, at the request of her father, she now directed her communication to Jane Addams. At the time, neither White knew of the *Survey* article. For seven typewritten pages, Miss White took exception to the accusations mentioned in the original leaflet, primarily those regarding forced child labor, and refuted them or explained them with authority.[103] If Joseph White was keenly aware of everything that happened on the farm, Elizabeth White lived what happened on the farm. She describes her personal experience for Jane Addams.

> For 12 years I went to the fields with the pickers in the morning and stayed till the last one had left in the evening; I was scorched by the same sun, chilled by the same winds, wet by the same showers, and lived all day long in the same sweet air; to my great physical benefit.[104]

Shortly after Elizabeth sent her letter to Addams, J. J. White suffered a medical collapse that would keep him sidelined for six months and would force Elizabeth to step into his shoes. Although not yet an official member of the Cranberry Growers' Association, the members recognized her capabilities, and they accepted Elizabeth as one of the Association's spokespersons. In 1912, she accompanied Messrs. C. E. Budd, Newton Clevenger, and A. J. Rider, when they appeared as representatives of the growers before the New Jersey State Immigration Commission, during that group's investigation of the NCLC's accusations.

Rider, Secretary of the Growers' Association, reported back to the members during their Annual Convention, held in Mount Holly, on August 24, 1912. He also publicly acknowledged "Miss White's ability and experience along these lines" and allotted her a slot in the program. At the end of White's comments on Housing and Care of Cranberry Pickers, the official minutes remark that her sentiments were heartily applauded.[105] She would address the growers again on this subject more than once over the years.

That first visit Lewis Hine and Edward Brown made to the New Jersey bogs in 1910 opened the door to inspections by many and varied agencies. The National Child Labor Committee returned in 1911 and 1913, each time reporting that little to nothing had been done to rectify the situation. Reverend Augustine Elmendorf, himself a member of the NCLC, visited the bogs in September 1914 on behalf of the New Jersey Episcopal Church. His evaluation was not nearly as harsh as that of the NCLC and did much to improve the growers' standing in official circles.[106] Later that same year, the New Jersey Child Labor Committee held yet another investigation. The three-person panel did not visit the bogs since the harvest season had ended and the pickers had gone. Instead, they held interviews and received testimony from Mr. Brown as a representative of the NCLC, the Reverend Elmendorf, and Cranberry Growers Association members Clifford Budd, A. J. Rider, and Elizabeth White. The group also contacted officials and teachers in the Philadelphia Public School System. The committee concluded that cooperation would accomplish more than laws. The panel recommended a conference be called, during which all appropriate social, heath, educational, and agricultural entities could be heard, and agreeable solutions reached. No known documentation exists to show that such a meeting ever occurred.

During all these inquiries, Elizabeth sought every opportunity to defend the cranberry growers. Her first major forum was the 1911 New Jersey Conference of Charities and Corrections, scheduled at Princeton University on April 2–4. The *Trenton Evening Times* well-publicized the gathering, beginning in January. By March, the *Times* reported "much interest" in the upcoming gathering. Elizabeth's presence was noted, as was her proposed address. The newspaper added that Miss White would have several photographic views illustrating her subject[107]when she delivered a paper titled, "A Short Report of the Cranberry Bog Situation." In it, White attempted to counteract the National Child Labor Committee's portrayal of picker working conditions on New Jersey's cranberry bogs. If attendees did not know or had forgotten the published details of "the Bog Situation," they could visit the NCLC's exhibit to become informed and, probably, incensed. From the discussion that followed White's speech, it is evident that the majority in the audience held no sympathy for the growers.

The NCLC immediately sought to reinforce its position by sending Charles Chute to re-visit bogs in Massachusetts and New Jersey during September 1911. Chute's evaluation was that in New Jersey nothing had changed except at the largest bog (White's), where the grower had additional houses built and improved toilet facilities. Once again, *The Survey* article that reported his findings was entitled, "Cost of the Cranberry Sauce."[108] The use of that particular title had an adverse impact on sales, as intended. The economic barrage against the growers continued with Campbell MacCulloch's November 1913 feature in *Good Housekeeping* magazine entitled, "Who Picked Your Cranberries?" In an introduction prior to the article, MacCulloch embellished on Lovejoy's original picture of the number of children affected.

> Philadelphia has slums and poverty; New Jersey has cranberry-bogs and men willing to hire the little children of the poor. The result is that between five and six thousand children from two school districts in Philadelphia do not return to school until late in the fall.[109]

He further inflamed the situation with an illustration of a small girl picking cranberries, with the caption asking if this little one was working to provide the family Thanksgiving treat while their daughter was enjoying a day in school. It would be logical to assume that cranberry sales would suffer.

The next opportunity Elizabeth White had to address a large assembly was again during a New Jersey Conference of Charities and Correction, held at Asbury Park, New Jersey, during April 1914. She arrived well prepared, delivering a paper that was later published. In "Cranberries and Colony Contributions," White associated two seemingly diverse subjects, the condition of the Italian women and children on the cranberry bogs of New Jersey and the establishment of Four Mile Colony of the Vineland Training School. Throughout the speech, she compares the opposing perspective regarding child labor between the NCLC and the Training School.[110] There are also statements refuting specific charges against the growers. Perhaps the most surprising element in this paper is Elizabeth's attack on the methods the NCLC sometimes used to achieve its goals, honorable as they may be. White's remarks were well-received by many. There are ten letters in the Whitesbog archives attesting to this fact. Some were from cranberry farmers, of course, but there were also praises from interested citizens.

On December 21, 1914, the *Trenton Evening Times* reported that the "cranberry dispute" between NCLC and South Jersey growers was finally ending. The previous week, Owen Lovejoy had released a detailed letter admitting errors in the original presentation of conditions on the bogs; many were the very issues he refused to yield to J. J. White in 1910. But Lovejoy was adamant in maintaining the NCLC's concern over the indisputable facts of children still engaged in picking cranberries and missing school during the harvest, and of the poor housing conditions. In the same newspaper article, former State Senator Everett Colby is cited as saying he believed the letter would result in the disappearance of old soreness. Elizabeth White, described in the article as the "moving spirit" of the cranberry growers' association, had apparently predicted that if Mr. Lovejoy would issue such a statement, the cranberry growers would probably appoint a committee at their next convention to confer with the child labor organizations on ways and means for bettering conditions.[111]

While she was totally pro-growers in public appearances, Elizabeth White and other growers knew there was a kernel of truth in the accusations. She shared the experience of the 1914 harvest inspection by Rev. Augustine Elmendorf with those present at the annual meeting of the American Cranberry Growers Association on January 25, 1915. After she had reported on the visit, Elizabeth presented four improvements that the Reverend recommended, which he felt would go a long way to appeasing the critics. These changes were improved housing; providing more sanitary and separate men/women toilet facilities, protection of the water supply, and the elimination of standing water to reduce flies and mosquitoes. Elizabeth continued:

> In accordance with this suggestion, Mr. Rider, Mr. George Holman and myself, as an informal committee representing three widely separated cranberry districts, have drawn up the following outline as embodying

what seem to us the best practices of our respective districts.[112]

She then presented the fleshed-out plan and suggested that it be adopted by the Association. Elmendorf's gentler assessment, along with Lovejoy's retraction, apparently made the Association amenable to accepting the proposal. Mr. James Holman moved that the report be printed in the minutes, and that the Association endorse the plans as recommended. The motion passed.[113]

By the early 1920s, most farms had switched to scoop picking; children still came with their families, but their presence on the bogs proved less problematic. It appeared that the issue had been laid to rest, but this was not the case. At the annual meeting in 1930, the year White served as President, the group passed a resolution, stating its desire to be ethical in conducting its business.[114] The members resolved to petition the New Jersey State Board of Agriculture to conduct a survey of the following issues: absence from school, hiring children under sixteen at any time of the year, the economic situations of both employer and employee when such hiring was done, and general working conditions. The Board would publish its findings so that abuses could be eliminated.[115]

A year later, at the next annual meeting, Harry Weiss, Secretary of the Commission to Investigate the Employment of Migratory Children in the State of New Jersey, presented the survey results to all present. The first thing reported was a list of reasons for the necessity of hiring migrant workers for all agricultural crops. He followed this with a statistical compilation of basic facts, such as the number of families/individuals participating in New Jersey migratory agriculture, average financial status per family, and housing conditions at both the farm and family home. Space, sanitation, water supply, and schooling came up short on the growers' side. Members responded by asking questions and offering insights. Mr. Weiss indicated an urgency in the situation. "The National Child Labor Committee is threatening action, probably to keep the work going. They sometimes think that children are being exploited. By that word, they mean 'working'."[116] Sixteen years after the *Trenton Times* reported the "Cranberry Dispute Will End," the cranberry farmers and the NCLC continued sparring.

Although immersed in blueberry experimentation and commercialization throughout that time span, Elizabeth White made time to address two of the major complaints of the Committee, education and housing.

Lewis W. Hine's photographs at Whitesbog

Lewis W. Hine made the following images during his visit to Whitesbog with Edward Brown in 1910. The two men were investigating working conditions for the National Child Labor Committee. These and other Whitesbog images are readily available through the digital collections of the Library of Congress.

Smallest girl is Rosie. Carries cranberries. Whites Bog, Brown Mills, N.J. This is the fourth week of school in Philadelphia, and the people here expect to remain here two weeks more. September 28, 1910. *Courtesy of Library of Congress.* All captions from Library of Congress records.

Teresa Lerre, 5 years old, cranberry picker. 1024 9th St., Philadelphia. The father and four children are picking. A "carrier" may be seen at one side. Whites Bog, Browns Mills, N.J. September 1910. *Courtesy of Library of Congress.*

Frances Frigineto, 3 years old. Marie Frigineto, 5 years old, latter been picking two years. 711 Patchionk Ave., Philadelphia. Whites Bog, Brown Mills, N.J. Witness E. F. Brown. September 1910. *Courtesy of Library of Congress.*

A group of cranberry pickers moving from one part of the bog to another. Whites Bog, Browns Mills, N.J. Sept. 28, 1910. Witness E. F. Brown. *Courtesy of Library of Congress.*

Millie Cornaro, Philadelphia, 10 years old. Been picking cranberries for 6 years. White's Bog, Browns Mills, N. J. This is the fourth week of school and the people here expect to remain here two weeks more. Sept. 28, 1910. Witness, E. F. Brown." *Courtesy of Library of Congress.*

Victoria Borsa, 1223 Catherine St., Philadelphia. 4-year-old berry picker. Brother 7 years old. While I was photographing them, the mother was impatiently urging them to "pick, pick." Whites Bog, Brown Mills, N.J. September 1910. *Courtesy of Library of Congress.*

Shack of Jo. Mermilla family, cranberry pickers on Whites Bog, Browns Mills, N.J in settlement called Florence. Six persons live in this room. One bed on floor. Food exposed to flies, etc., on rafters and on floor. The children were very dirty and ill-kept. E. F. Brown Witness. September 1910. *Courtesy of Library of Congress.*

Room 75, Shanty 4, Cranberry pickers Paulo Biniristo and wife live here. Settlement called Rome, on Whites Bog, Browns Mills, N.J. 4 sons live in next room. Note the bread and other food lying around unprotected. Plenty of flies. E. F. Brown Witness. *Courtesy of Library of Congress.*

Teresa Lamelli, 818 Kate St., Philadelphia, 5 years old. Whites Bog, Browns Mills, N.J. Sept. 28, 1910. Witness E. F. Brown. *Courtesy of Library of Congress.*

Rose Biodo, 1216 Annan St., Philadelphia. 10 years old. Working 3 summers. Minds baby and carries berries, two pecks at a time. Whites Bog, Brown Mills, N.J. Sept. 28, 1910. Witness E. F. Brown." *Courtesy of Library of Congress.*

Salvin Nocito, 5 years old, carries 2 pecks of cranberries for long distance to the "bushel-man." Whites Bog, Browns Mills, N.J. Sept. 28, 1910. Witness E. F. Brown. *Courtesy of Library of Congress.*

Addressing Needs:
Education

The National Child Labor Committee's assessment of conditions on the White plantation was that workers were being treated very well overall. This is what Elizabeth knew; she may have naively thought other growers mirrored the White environment on each cranberry farm. It *was*, on those of growers with whom her family associated closely. Perhaps the investigations raised an unbidden awareness that Elizabeth felt obligated to explore. A major complaint of the committee was that by the children of migrant Italian laborers participating in the cranberry harvest, they surrendered their right to education, particularly during the critical beginning weeks of the school year.

An immediate response on the part of the Whites was to offer children of pickers the opportunity to attend Whitesbog's school, which was part of the public school system. Based on available school attendance records, it appears that only a very few families took advantage of the offer. In 1915, Elizabeth reached out to the National Congress of Mother and Parent-Teacher Associations. A response from the President, Mrs. Frederic Schoff, expressed support for the growers' situation. She writes: ". . . many of the thinking people in this country feel that the movement to protect children from injurious work is going to the extreme of preventing them from all opportunities of work and is placing a great handicap on parents."[117]

Education for the children of migrant agricultural workers was an issue before the attack on the cranberry farmers and continued long after. While attending the Hoover Housing Conference in 1931, it appears White sought out delegates connected to education. Her program from the event shows the names of two women and their associated schools penciled on the front cover. Since neither attended the conference, it is assumed that one of the other attendees, possibly another member of the Migrant Worker Housing Subcommittee, thought Elizabeth would benefit from contacting them.

Around the same time, Elizabeth attended a migrant education conference sponsored by the Maryland Conference of the League of Women Voters. The official invitees included the NCLC and the heads of Departments of Labor and Education—all professionals in the field. There were also the off-the-record attendees—people like Elizabeth White who held a passionate interest in education and agriculture. Three years before the Housing Conference, Elizabeth initiated a project that would last about a decade. Over the years, she recommended steps that could be taken to improve the lot of the migrants, particularly the Italian families who came in droves from South Philadelphia.

The Italian mothers often had a difficult time juggling their several duties. They needed to pick to make the journey to the bogs worthwhile monetarily, but, in many cases, they also needed to care for small children at the same time, making both tasks very stressful. The easiest solution was to take the children into the field with them, thereby setting up the stage for the child labor issue. In 1928, Elizabeth White acted to alleviate this one aspect of such a demanding occupation. She invited the Council of Women for Home Missions to establish a daycare facility at Whitesbog. It is unknown who initiated negotiations. Elizabeth might have made the first contact or perhaps the Council communicated with her, since the organization already had a presence in migrant camps among truck farms and fisheries in New Jersey. All was ready for their arrival until one family, already exposed to diphtheria, arrived for the cranberry harvest. For safety's sake, plans were cancelled until 1929. The group went to Theodore Budd's farm instead, undoubtedly on Elizabeth White's recommendation.

Who were the Women of Home Missions and what did they see as their role in the cranberry industry? The Council of Women for Home Missions was formed in 1908 "to unify the efforts of the national Women's Home Mission boards of the United States . . . by consultation and cooperation in action."[118] Among the migrant labor force, they wanted to create "essential programs to provide worship, religious education, spiritual and moral guidance, recreation and certain health and welfare sources. However, since the individual is indivisible, all problems that affect him must be our concern."[119]

When 1929 arrived, it was Whitesbog's turn. What follows is an extract from a detailed hand-written diary kept by the three women who came that first year.

While the account that follows does not reflect direct involvement of Elizabeth White from a hands-on perspective, the program would never have materialized without her efforts. The description of the first year's experience also makes the "migrant" issue a human one.

September 8, 1929, was a Sunday. Lois, Helen, and Pauline drove into Whitesbog and then were directed to Florence, the housing settlement for the Italian pickers. One of the three women possessed experience as a missionary; at least one of the other two was preparing to be a teacher. The children were jubilant: the nurses had arrived; tomorrow they would go to the Casa. By "the Casa," they meant the nursery building erected sometime prior. Sunday was a busy day for the three women as they settled in and then inspected what would be their workplace for the next month and a half. The nursery contained three rooms that suited their needs to accommodate three groupings of children: infants, pre-school, and kindergarten. With the help of a few older girls, they whipped the nursery into shape, including wiping down the tables, chairs, shelves and cabinets, while some men installed mosquito netting. Youngsters milled about watching every step of the procedure. Some would come to the center, while others would be cared for by their own families.

Monday, September 9, 1929. The adventure began, as did many accompanying challenges. Thirty-six children arrived, among them seven infants, but the nursery contained only four baskets that could serve as cribs. Ten more little ones under the age of three years came and they required as much care as the infants.

The remainder ranged in age from three to nine. Following the NCLC investigation, farm rules prohibited children under ten from being on the bogs. One of the first things the "nurses" did was to order twelve quarts of milk. Noise seemed to be the general characteristic of that first day. According to Lois' account, fifteen of their charges cried all day, stopping only long enough to eat. Certainly an understandable cacophony arose, with the little ones thrust into unfamiliar surroundings and into the care of strangers who spoke a strange language. Howls instead of music accompanied finger plays (perhaps itsy bitsy spider?). With the day beginning about eight in the morning, the appearance of parents around 5:30 p.m. to collect their children was a welcome sight to the three women.

On day three, Lois, Helen, and Pauline instituted a regular program schedule. The first item of the day going forward was the cleanliness routine, comprising the toothbrush drill, face and hand washing, and hair combing. For many of the children, this seemed to be a new experience, especially brushing their teeth. They had never seen a toothbrush and promptly ate the toothpaste.

The Council had established the standard program guidelines the women followed as a proven methodology in migrant camps. The children's day ran something like this:

- The Cleanliness Routine.
- Salute the Flags—both national and Christian.
- Circle Talk followed with all the children. This was basically a time of religious instruction.

- Songs, prayers (repeated or initiated by the children), a Bible story or a story to illustrate good character.
- Division into age groupings where telling stories, sharing of home life or other experiences, handwork such as coloring, drawing, or making puppets occurred.
- Lunch—a three-part activity. Children helped to prepare by clearing the tables where they had been working and learning how to set them for eating. No one had to teach them how to enjoy their meal, although there were lessons in good manners. Finally, the children cleaned up after lunch, which, in most cases, was quite a learning process.
- Quiet time came next in the order of the day to give the children a nap.
- Outdoor games and stories filled the remainder of the children's time together. The abundance of sand made for a good time if a child was lucky enough to gain possession of a bucket and shovel. (After a few years, nature studies using cranberries, blueberries, and Pineland plants as subject matter periodically replaced game time. It is possible that Elizabeth White suggested this change, since she had advocated environmental studies for seasonal children from the beginning of the labor controversy.)

In the early days of NCLC scrutiny, the committee alleged that the children suffered from malnourishment when they returned from the bogs. No one could make such an accusation about the children under the care of the Home Mission ladies. They cooked as well as taught and served nutritious meals of vegetable soup, bean soup, spaghetti, milk and, always, lots and lots of bread and butter. When the Italian pickers first began coming, Whitesbog had its own bakery. Bread was one of the best-selling items in the General Store. That was around 1908. No written record tells us if the bakery survived until 1929, but, by all accounts, bread was still a popular item in the store. Cost for the food was covered in part by the workers who were asked to pay ten cents a day if their children attended the center and by the monies allocated to the project by the Council.

As the first three missionaries drove into the village, the children said the nurses had arrived. In addition to being teachers and cooks five and a half days a week, the women had this one last calling—nurse on demand. Children with minor, and sometimes not so minor, cuts and ailments arrived for care. The women treated cuts, burns, infected wounds, and poison ivy. Sometimes they had to deal with more serious conditions like impetigo and head lice. When a case proved beyond their expertise, the women saw to it that the person received proper medical care. Because they lived among the workers, nursing hours went beyond the normal eight-to-five day.

Veteran Whitesbog pickers had become accustomed to the company addressing their medical needs. J. J. White was a pioneer in offering health benefits to his employees. Joseph J. White, Inc., secured the services of a doctor, who visited the farm every two weeks for a contracted fee. Workers with a medical problem could see the doctor and individually paid him fifty cents per visit. On any given day, if the sum of the individual consultations did not reach the contracted fee, the company paid the difference. Elizabeth had taken a first aid course, enabling her to provide care for minor ills between doctor visits.

J. J. took pride in his daughter's training and referred to it in one of his letters to Owen Lovejoy of the National Child Labor Committee. When Elizabeth built her home in Whitesbog, she included a dispensary for treating workers. Finally, the cranberry picking season ended. As Lois, Helen, and Pauline packed up equipment and materials, they had to look back with satisfaction at what they had accomplished. Despite the challenges of language barriers, sometimes demanding mothers, and lack of equipment, the women had provided care for body, mind, and soul, thereby remaining true to their missionary role. It was October 17, 1929.[120] Elizabeth White served as President of the American Growers Cranberry Association from August 1929 until August 1930. She concluded the Presidential Address, which completed her term, with a recap of Whitesbog's first experience with the Council of Women for Home Missions.

Many of you know that last summer the Council of Women for Home Missions operated at Whitesbog a day nursery and a kindergarten for the care and teaching of the babies and little children. A similar center was also conducted on Theodore Budd's bog. That was a help to everybody. The children were better off, the mothers and big boys and girls could do better work when free of the responsibility for the tots, and those who were doing the managing found it much easier without the children under foot.

I think this is the germ from which such education as I visualize would have to grow. Last summer the girls conducting the center were leaders in games and recreation for the older children when they were not working. It kept them interested and out of mischief and, with further development, might easily be more educational.

Contributions to the Women's Council for Home Missions are deductible from income for Income Tax purposes. I made a personal contribution last season and expect to contribute more heavily this year. I trust many of you may do likewise and thus assist in putting the work for the education of these children on a permanently high plane.[121]

The Women of the Home Missions returned to Whitesbog each year for both the blueberry and cranberry harvests until the early 1940s. Programs expanded for all the children of migrant families. Use of the former barrel factory provided recreational opportunities to the older crowd in the form of movies and shuffleboard games.

The Home Mission was not the only presence at Whitesbog during the 1931 season. A group of New Jersey citizens sponsored a research fellowship to determine to what extent the educational and welfare needs of migrant workers' children were being met while their parents engaged in cultivating or harvesting crops. The research also included an investigation of the same children's home and educational conditions when back in the cities during the winter months. The study was conducted at Whitesbog and in Philadelphia. Rutgers

University directed and supervised the study. Miss Laura Fair, a graduate student who had had experience with migrant children and training as a social worker, received the fellowship funding.

When Miss Fair completed her investigation, Rutgers published the results, which indicated that, from an educational standpoint, the children would have fared better if circumstances did not require them to accompany their parents to the fields.[122] The findings also showed, however, that their school work did not suffer as much as previously alleged or feared. The final topic in the study report provided several suggestions for educational approaches in migrant areas. Some would require state support and cooperation between school districts. No documentation exists in the archives to indicate that Whitesbog acted on these suggestions, except for continued company support for the Women of the Home Missions. On a personal level, Elizabeth must have forged a friendship with Laura Fair, since we find a bequest left to her in White's will.

The topic of education came up in totally different circumstances during this same period. Elizabeth Kite approached the Whites regarding the new Vineland colony, which would involve the education of developmentally challenged young men. At the same time, Kite was advocating for reform in New Jersey's educational system, particularly as it affected rural communities. Kite's proposals piqued Elizabeth White's interest. She soon found herself enmeshed on all three scholastic arenas: rural issues, the Training School, and providing educational opportunities for children of migrant workers.

Most state governments failed to make rural education a priority. In Elizabeth's time, New Jersey appropriated educational funds based on attendance. Neighborhood schools in urban centers seldom closed due to inclement weather, whereas severe winter weather or spring planting and the fall harvest often closed far-flung schools in farming communities. In 1915, L. L. Gratz, Superintendent of the Pemberton School District, reported that during the 1911–1912 school year, 5,000 student attendance days were lost. That winter had been especially snowy and the road between the Coates school and Lemontown had been closed for five weeks. Without sufficient funding, school districts found it impossible to hire good teachers or maintain proper school buildings.

The same situation existed at the Four Mile School (the local public school, not associated with the Vineland Colony at Four Mile). The district forced one young woman who served as teacher out of town when it became evident that she failed to fulfill her obligations and blatantly flaunted her loose sexual morals. The school had no heat, few books, totally inadequate toilet facilities, and only a rusted pail for drinking water.

Elizabeth became aware of the students' plight through Sarah Macomber, the wife of Four Mile Colony Manager, J. Frank Macomber. Mrs. Macomber had stepped in to provide some basic education. She contacted the local school board to have some improvements made to the building, but received a response that conditions at Four Mile School was as good as any other. Elizabeth was not satisfied with the status quo at the school. In the winter of 1915, she addressed the

Daughters of the American Revolution at a meeting in Trenton. During her speech, she recounted the plight of Mrs. Macomber and Four Mile. Elizabeth made two requests to her fellow DAR members. Of course, she asked them for monetary help to alleviate the immediate need. More importantly, she urged these women to help *all* rural students in New Jersey by working to effect change to the way in which the state distributed funds.

Elizabeth sought to be involved in local education in a very personal way. She ran for a seat on the Pemberton Township School Board in 1911 and 1913, but lost both elections. On a familial level, when she learned that her cousin's husband died in the Johnstown flood, she oversaw the education of three of the couple's children. Thanks to her, a teacher, a nurse, and a musician became contributing members of society. In one final example of Elizabeth White's passion for education and outreach, she began to support teaching missionaries. The devastation resulting from World War I left many orphans in Syria. Various global Christian agencies dispatched missionaries to provide care and schooling, including Daniel and Emily Oliver. The couple opened an orphanage in Ras-el-Metn, located in a section of Syria that later became Lebanon. It is unclear how Elizabeth became aware of their work, but it might have been through her Philadelphia contacts, since the Olivers were Quakers and their foundation was headquartered in Philadelphia. What we do know is that she became one of their sponsors until the day she died. On a poignant note, she never received the last thank you and Christmas greeting card, dated November 30, 1954. Elizabeth had gone to her reward on November 27.

Addressing Needs:
Housing

Another concern of the National Child Labor Committee was the deplorable housing conditions they found on some of the bogs. The committee deemed the accommodations on White's farm acceptable, but these must not have been the norm. The Cranberry Growers Association had enough concern to establish a three-person task force to examine the situation and make suitable recommendations. The committee consisted of George Holman of Ocean County, Elizabeth White of Burlington County, and Andrew Rider of Atlantic County. The committee members represented all the cranberry growing areas and the members took into consideration the varying conditions in each. Elizabeth served as the spokesperson for the group when they presented their findings at the 1915 meeting of the association. These were relatively simple: single storied houses, good drinking water, and adequate sanitation. Some growers readily accepted the changes; others did not, claiming that the number of pickers was declining due to the use of scooping, rather than hand picking.

The same year that the Women of Home Missions came to Whitesbog, the Great Depression came to the people of the United States. Many looked to the federal government for relief, which was not forthcoming. The nation blamed President Herbert Hoover for the terrible economic and social conditions. As unemployment spread, so did home eviction. Shantytowns appeared across the U.S., primarily on the outskirts of major cities. In derision, they became known as Hoovervilles. The President believed that self-reliance and self-help, not government intervention, would provide the best means to meet citizens' needs and could be applied to the housing problem. A Conference on Home Ownership and Home Building, the second in the series of social studies, following one on Child Health and Protection, was announced on August 30, 1930.

On September 15, 1931, the President announced a follow-up conference to be held during December in Washington, D.C., and the reasoning behind it:

> I decided a year ago after a conference with interested leaders in various parts of the country to undertake the organization of an adequate investigation and study, on a nationwide scale, of the problems presented in homeownership and homebuilding, with the hope of developing the facts and a better understanding of the questions involved and inspiring better organization and the removal of influences which seriously limit the spread of homeownership, both town and country.[123]

The President's Conference on Home Ownership and Home Building convened on December 2, 1931, with more than 3,000 attendees. The conference spawned twenty-five fact-finding committees to study every aspect of housing needs and construction. Six additional committees were charged with the task of correlating the results of the research and formulating recommendations in administration, legislation, technology and the like. More than 540 volunteers worked for a year gathering data and preparing reports. Elizabeth White was invited to be one of these and to serve on the Farm and Village Housing Committee, more specifically, the subcommittee dedicated to the Housing of Migratory Labor. No documentation has been found to indicate who suggested her inclusion. One possibility was a member of the Conference's Planning Committee, Lillian Gilbreth of Montclair, New Jersey,[124] who must have been aware of White's role in the Child Labor controversy.

The individual committees presented their reports over a three-day period. Elizabeth had been involved in preparing her sub-committee's seven recommendations and the points held a strong resemblance to the standards she, Andrew Rider, and Holman had advocated to the American Cranberry Growers Association in 1915. These included the basic needs of an adequate clean water supply, ground drainage to eliminate standing water, and proper sewage and garbage disposal. The recommendations paid special attention to the amount of space and air circulation allocated to each person. The committee placed utmost importance on the licensing and supervision of camps by an authorized state department.[125]

Despite Elizabeth's personal involvement in negotiating with the National Child Labor Committee, and her attempts to improve housing for seasonal workers on the bogs, as well as educational opportunities for their children, conditions at Whitesbog seemingly deteriorated over the years, particularly toward the end of the 1930s. At least, the Home Mission counselors held this impression, as noted in some of the end-of-season written reports. These narratives regularly addressed two issues: physical accommodations and wages. The 1939 Whitesbog Report contains this entry:

> The company tries to keep the workers satisfied, but it doesn't want to spend too much money. . . . The younger folks aren't as easily satisfied as the older ones. One young man acknowledged he loafed on the job since he was being paid so poorly.[126]

It was relatively easy for the Home Mission Workers to compare conditions and wages on different farms, since they had active projects in multiple locations and the workers visited each other on occasion. One worker wrote: "The wage level at Whitesbog seems to be set as low as it is possible to get enough help."[127] While J. J. White was paying 4 ½ – 5 ½ cents per quart of blueberries picked, Theodore Budd was paying 7 cents.

Requests for repairs or improvements were sometimes acted upon and sometimes not. The Home Mission workers had gradually expanded their programs to include activities for older children and adults. In 1937, Joseph J. White, Inc., after making renovations, gave them use of the building known as the Barrel Factory[128] for gatherings, showing movies, and other activities. The floor sported a newly painted shuffleboard court and management provided a ping-pong table to offer other recreational outlets. The installation of a jukebox was a welcome addition. Dances were the activity of choice for the teenage set. In 1938, Joseph J. White, Inc., received a request for a metal fence around the nursery in Florence. A wooden fence already existed, but it required constant repair. Workers, too lazy to chop the logs provided to fuel the wood stoves, constantly stole slats from the fence. A repeat appeal for the fence in 1939 indicates the company failed to honor the original request.

Not every report about Whitesbog was negative. While almost all documentation regarding the Home Mission Council's work at Whitesbog refers to the Italian laborers who occupied the Florence settlement, the missionaries also had concerns for the workers who lived in Rome, the older of the two housing complexes at Whitesbog. By the late 1930s, Rome served as a residential area for workers composed primarily of older Portuguese men, along with a black community. In a publication that summarized the 1942 experience in all of New Jersey, Whitesbog's Rome settlement is specifically mentioned. "One of the most satisfying outcomes of the year's work at Whitesbog is the establishment of a church at Rome. A group of Negroes, regular churchgoers in other towns, hungered for a church 'on the bogs'."[129] They found a little eight by ten room in an old storage barn. Elizabeth White gave them permission to use it and the residents established a church there. The Reverend C. H. Richmond came from the council's farm camp in Burlington, New Jersey, to conduct services. Of that occasion, Pastor Richmond said, "It is the most inspiring place that I have ever preached."[130]

At the end of the 1942 blueberry season, the Home Mission Council presented Joseph J. White, Inc., with a set of three demands. If the company failed to meet these demands before the cranberry picking season began, the Council would not return.

> 1. The White company had to supply the Center (Daycare) with adequate physical facilities: an indoor toilet, a stove and lighting for autumn, and sufficient tables.
> 2. Adequate housing for the pickers.
> 3. A pay scale that matched the going rate on other bogs.[131]

This is the very last entry in the Home Mission Archives regarding Whitesbog, so it appears the mission did not return.

Going back to the 1939 Report, we also find a positive aspect of the employer-employee relationship. "The pickers on the whole have a good feeling toward the company. In fact, those who have been coming back year after year for fifteen years or so feel that they are a part of the place." And with respect to Elizabeth herself:

> The main contact with the company is through Elizabeth White who has lived at Whitesbog for a very long time. She has always been very interested in the workers, and it is really thru' her efforts that they enjoy as good conditions as they have now. All of the workers respect her very highly. This fact was brought home very strongly one evening when she spoke at the Barrel House about the development of the cultivated

blueberry. Although announcement of her talk was not given out until that afternoon, a crowded house was here to hear Miss White speak; that turn-out was really a tribute to her, because I know many of those older women probably did not understand much of what she had to say.[132]

Without access to both financial records and meeting minutes, involving intensive research, it is impossible to determine the reasons underlying the seeming change in philosophy on the part of Joseph J. White, Inc. The following circumstances are offered to the reader to help consider the opposite side of the coin. An atmosphere of worker discontent appears to have emerged concomitantly with the world undergoing significant turmoil. The United States was just emerging from the Great Depression; Europe was facing a devastating war that would spread to the entire globe.

By 1942, the U.S. labor force would be decimated. Agricultural managers had to compete for farm workers with higher paying war-related jobs. Whitesbog was one of the farms caught in the tussle. The United States became a huge customer for cranberries during World War II. The dried fruit was an excellent and easily carried nutritional source for troops overseas. The financial impact of having the government as a major customer on any grower, not just Whitesbog, has not been part of the research for this account. Added to the outside influences, internally, company President Frank Chambers suffered from declining health. The company faced the future with an aging board of directors and lacking a viable immediate successor for Chambers.

What the company needed was another J. J. White for a new era.

Four Mile Colony

A knock at the door, an invitation to join the family at dinner: thus began the forging of a long-lasting commitment and a lifetime friendship. The year was 1912 and the White family welcomed Elizabeth S. Kite to their table. During that dinner conversation, they learned that Miss Kite was compiling the family histories of some children in Vineland. Elizabeth remembered the encounter.

> She had already done considerable work in our area and my mother and I were able to add to her list of names and characteristics of grandfathers and great-grandfathers, sisters, cousins and aunts; for the families she was studying had been our near neighbors for generations. Our family followed her work with the keenest interest through the months that followed. Through association with her we became interested in the Vineland work.[133]

What was this Vineland work? In 1880s New Jersey, no place existed to provide housing for "feeble-minded" children requiring care. In 1887, the Rev. Dr. Stephen Olin Garrison, a Methodist minister, responding to the need, embarked on the daunting journey of establishing a school where mentally challenged children would be taught and cared for in a creative and loving way. He began his venture in his own home in Millville, New Jersey, but, by the end of a year, as word of his experiment spread, the requests for admission amounted to more than could be accommodated in the small space. Philanthropist B. D. Maxham offered Garrison the Scarborough Mansion and 40 acres in Vineland, New Jersey. In 1888, Garrison's school officially opened with 55 children. The original name of the school at its founding was "The New Jersey Home for the Education and Care of Feebleminded Children." By the time Elizabeth Kite met the White family, the name had been changed to "The Training School at Vineland."

By 1910, some of the boys who first came to Vineland had become grown men and had completed their learning at that facility. Additionally, the presence of adult males there presented social issues that had to be addressed, since the school's residents comprised both male and female. Dr. Edward R. Johnstone, who had succeeded Dr. Garrison as head of the school, decided to establish a small farm nearby for some of the men and to teach them to be more self-sufficient through agriculture and animal husbandry. It would be located close to the Vineland school so that he could supervise its progress closely. The new facility would continue "The Cottage Plan" Garrison first introduced, which involved residential small group homes, instead of large dormitories. Johnstone called the new facility the Menantico Colony and the experiment worked well.

In 1913, as more young boys matured into men, Dr. Johnstone felt it was time to replicate Menantico for the next group of Vineland graduates. This time, he chose Burlington County as the location. The State of New Jersey had agreed to donate the land and a meager food allowance per resident, but the rest of the Colony's expenses would be Vineland's responsibility. A search began for the appropriate location within Lebanon State Forest before selecting the Four Mile site. In the summer of 1913, Johnstone thought it time to present his idea to the locals. Elizabeth Kite had laid the groundwork. She had visited the families with children in the Vineland school for background and to assess their experience with the institution. Kite had also garnered the support of "interested" parties, such as the White Family. A meeting took place in Pemberton at the home of Mrs. John C. Fremont. Those present included J. J. White and Elizabeth, Mrs. Strawbridge-Brophy of Moorestown, and Mrs. Fremont.[134] From this small group began the organization that would launch the Four Mile Colony. For Elizabeth, personally, this work began a major commitment that would last for the ensuing thirty years.

Later that fall, she joined with many other Burlington County citizens who assembled at the Burlington High School to hear about the project. Professor Johnstone, Miss Kite, and Mr. Joseph P. Byers, New Jersey Commissioner of Charities and Corrections, presented the plans for the new colony, but also recounted its many needs. Johnstone had land and food, but no buildings to house the men. This was clearly the most urgent need and required money for construction. The community responded; the meeting spawned committees to address publicity, fund raising, and other aspects of the project.

As the public organized their efforts, Dr. Johnstone initiated a search for the right person to lead and manage the colony. He and Elizabeth Kite met at Whitesbog to consider the question when Miss Kite suggested the Macombers.

J. Frank Macomber had worked at Vineland for several years as purchaser and store manager. His wife, Sara Denney Macomber, was a trained nurse. Both had proven to be trustworthy, caring individuals. They would be a very good choice for Four Mile Colony.

The Macombers settled in during the winter of 1913–1914. The weather was severe and the rude accommodations provided only the sparsest of shelter. Mr. Macomber's diary entry of January 18, 1914, noted that both he and his wife had bronchitis and that Mr. Joseph White and Miss Elizabeth White came to call. Knowing the White family's sense of hospitality and neighborliness, J. J. and Elizabeth undoubtedly arrived with gifts that would fill the newcomers' larder.

Slowly, and with many challenges, the construction of the first cottage moved forward. As the men attended to the structural aspects of establishing the Colony, it became evident that Mrs. Macomber would need assistance with attending to the personal needs of the young men who would be arriving. The Board of Lady Visitors was formed with Elizabeth White as its president. These women were "hands on" kind of people who would get things accomplished. They traveled to Four Mile regularly to assess conditions for themselves.

It soon became evident that they needed an income source to achieve their goals and to contribute to the overall project. Together with the Macombers, they planned "Colony Picnics," inviting the citizens of Burlington County to bring box lunches and stay for the day. The first was held in July 1915. In the morning, the residents entertained the visitors and, in the afternoon, the young men played a baseball game. The colonists had also built a tennis court for the visitors to use. The last item on the day's agenda was a presentation of the progress made, the needs still not met, and a request for donations or subscriptions. Elizabeth had also suggested that people become members of a support group with a dollar-a-year membership fee. At this time, the colony provided shelter to thirty-two residents.[135] Burlington County citizens financed and supported Four Mile Colony. They had hoped the other counties of New Jersey would respond in a similar manner in caring for its mentally disadvantaged men and boys, but they did not.

Four Mile along with the Vineland Training School and its Menantico Colony offered the only such facilities in the state and students from all parts of New Jersey sought admittance. As the numbers grew at Four Mile, so did the need for more housing and, of course, funds to build, but the folks of Burlington County had nothing more to give. And so, after only two years, Four Mile Colony of the Vineland Training School became a state institution known as the "New Jersey State Colony for Boys," even though many of its residents were young men. It is likely that during this period of time, many referred to these grown men as "boys" in reference to their mental acuity and often childlike behavior. Frank Macomber remained on staff as manager. The existing Board of Directors and the

Board of Lady Visitors formally disbanded, although their interest as neighbors continued.

The state appointed a Board of Managers, and Elizabeth C. White became a member and remained active in this post until 1949, after which she was named a member emeritus until her death. At varying times over the span of thirty years, Elizabeth served as board secretary and vice-president.

In the spring of 1923, younger boys began to populate the Four Mile facility. Frank Macomber tendered his resignation the same year. The colony contained about 150 boys and men when he left, and Secretary White sang his praises well and loudly in the formal minutes of the Board of Managers. Macomber remained in the local area; he and his wife operated a boarding house for summer visitors in New Lisbon. During the remainder of the year, he busied himself with carpentry, remodeling houses, and building packing houses for the blueberry growers.[136] Macomber must have stayed in contact with the White family throughout, for in both 1925 and 1929, he engaged in property negotiations with the four sisters regarding land included in the Fenwick Manor holdings. He purchased a small plot from them in 1929 with the stipulation that if he ever decided to sell it, they would have the right of first refusal to buy it back. That happened in 1937.[137] At this time, Frank and Sarah Macomber likely moved to California, where they remained the rest of their lives. Between 1923 and 1929, the population of the Colony grew to 800. Sheer numbers alone would dictate altering the tenor of the institution, but another factor came into play. The New Jersey State Colony for Boys fell under the aegis of the New Jersey Commissioner of Charities and Corrections. As such, it not only served as a haven for the learning challenged, but also a depository for youth charged with criminal behavior, or as a last resort for hard-to-place orphans or runaways.

Many problems must have arisen, but the state archives have few detailed reports from the commissioner regarding the New Lisbon facility, when compared to notes on other institutions. Amid several items regarding mundane issues like equipment placement and menu changes, one account tells about the escape of six residents who stole a car along the way. The authorities caught three of the fugitives, but the other three remained at large. Within ten days, Commissioner Ellis called Mr. Cole, President of the Board, to schedule a meeting. At the end of that same year, Ellis called two special meetings of the board and made a personal visit to the institution. Another entry speaks of food distribution, based on the ability to work on the farm. Those who could work would require more sustenance; the feebler received less. An October 1931 visit to the Colony showed that the cafeteria left much to be desired. A suggestion was made to taste the food before serving and to give the little ones more milk. The Board of Managers raised additional concerns.

In August 1931, Elizabeth White requested a one-on-one meeting with Commissioner William J. Ellis, but nothing further could be learned about the meeting, not even a hint regarding the session's subject. This entry was followed by a notation about a meeting with Miss White, Mrs. Cole, Mrs. Newcomb and the appropriations committee, which was described as "quite an interesting conference on parole[138] and sterilization."[139] Again, an ambiguous portrayal, which serves only to pique both curiosity and thoughtful consideration. What position did Elizabeth take and what were her concerns on each topic? There is nothing in her surviving manuscripts that provides insight into the matter.

One cannot ignore the good things happening at the Colony. The first residents had helped in clearing the land and building the cottages. Work was always part of life in the Colony, but not the primary focus of the program. Professor Johnstone's rule was "Happiness First." The residents had a sense of accomplishment in seeing their living quarters erected with their own hands. Some gained joy in helping Mrs. Macomber with her garden or in learning to swim under her tutelage. As the Colony grew, the opportunities to learn new things also grew. What began as Occupational Therapy activities, such as basket weaving, expanded into furniture making, broom making, and all sorts of weaving used for rugs and clothing, making industrial arts one aspect of training at the Colony. The agricultural prowess of the residents also grew. Records in the state archives indicate that the New Lisbon Center contributed to the food supply of other state institutions.

Regular classroom education was not neglected for those residents who found themselves at New Lisbon for reasons other than learning difficulties. At some point, students from Antioch College arrived to teach the basics at Four Mile Colony. Antioch's philosophy was classroom instruction reinforced through a type of internship. This program resulted in the instructors at Four Mile changing every few months, which did not work for the students at the colony. For most of its inhabitants, continuity was essential to the educative process. The concept of learning, followed by practical experience, however, must have appealed to Elizabeth. She became a life-long supporter of the college.

Social interaction with the community was an integral part of the Colony's philosophy from day one. The facility held an open house, an "Annual Day," the celebration that began with the first picnic. One of the more amusing activities at one program was a bed-making contest. The boys challenged any man in the audience to come up and beat them at the task. The outcome brought much laughter. Neighbors also joined the residents for the holidays. Mr. Macomber's diary had the following entry.

> December 23, 1922. Santa Claus Party this evening. Dr. and Mrs. Darlington and Miss White attended, etc. The cottages were all visited after the party, and the Decorations were all very lovely.[140]

The Macombers had a deep appreciation of the Pinelands beauty that surrounded them. In *The Quarterly* issued for October 1, 1922, Frank wrote, "The flora of the pines is practically unlimited in its species and varieties . . . each species more beautiful than the other."[141] The cottages—Pixie, Lupin, Lobelia, etc.— were named in tribute. Elizabeth White may have been instrumental in furthering this appreciation. It was her dream to landscape the Colony grounds using native plants. She did not have the time to do it herself, but she had a friend who did. Under Miss White's tutelage,

Elizabeth Kite oversaw beautifying the grounds. Kite left Four Mile at the end of April 1931, but she did her best to see the work continued. On May 3, 1931, she wrote the following:

> My dear Sister White, It seems quite impossible for it to have been only a week ago that we went into that marvelous tangle of cedar swamp growth in quest of helonias.[142] What a vision of loveliness it was! And your garden—it refreshes me just to think of it and the blissful restfulness of it all.
>
> Someway the days at the Colony saw more accomplished than I could have supposed possible. Dr. Jones and Mr. Atkinson both went out with me one afternoon and Mr. Moore another day with his whole class. Nothing could have shown the value of school discipline as the contrast I noted between the boys I used to rely on and this class used now to obedience. Dr. J has ordered that this work go on at such times as a truck is available and either Miss Steinbach or one of the teachers will go along. In this way many ends will be accomplished besides the transplanting.[143]

It is not known if the Colony retained a native-plant-only regimen, but the residents were diligent in the grounds' upkeep. In 1951, an eight-year old boy entered the New Lisbon facility. Here is his first impression:

> However oblivious I was to the significance of the day's events, I couldn't help but be enchanted by the acreage before me; it was alive and dotted with

vibrant floral colors. The trees and bushes were pruned to perfection, the entirety of the scene exuding an air of tranquility and complete peace.[144]

Elizabeth C. White the Naturalist:
The Beauty of the Pines

So very much in Elizabeth White's life connected her to nature and to the environment. Her life-long career in agriculture, her selection of photographic topics, her love of pine barren plants, the energy she poured into research, conservation, and education demonstrate this in an undeniable way. Her involvement in blueberries and cranberries have been discussed from the perspective of the practical, economic aspect of her life's work. Elizabeth also had an artistic side; her soul reveled in the overwhelming beauty that surrounded her in that small portion of New Jersey which the uninformed called barren. The following pages attempt to convey the sheer joy that Elizabeth found in the plants and environs of the New Jersey Pine Barrens.

Elizabeth's Garden

Your garden—it refreshes me just to think of it and the blissful restfulness of it all! [145]

Elizabeth White's Pine Barrens garden became known throughout the region. Many came to visit and enjoy its beauty. An article published in the January 30,

1938, edition of *The Trenton Sunday Times* announced a series of fundraising garden tours with Miss White's garden as one of the venues. The proceeds benefited St. Mary's Hall, a private Episcopal girls school in Burlington.[146]

What made the garden so special? Elizabeth tells us herself. "The charm of every garden depends largely on the happy relationship of its open spaces to trees, bushes and flower borders,"[147] and, of course, on the unique selection of trees, bushes and flowers. For her garden at Suningive, her home at Whitesbog, Elizabeth primarily chose species indigenous to the small area of the globe she called home. Why did she love the entire community of native plants? The answer is simple: her Grandfather, James Fenwick, and father, Joseph J. White. Elizabeth must have been very young, probably under five, when she received her first lesson from a doting grandfather.

> The great pear tree was full of bloom and bees and spicy fragrance that sunny afternoon years ago when Grandfather Fenwick called his little granddaughter to see what he had brought her from "the bog."
>
> There . . . in grandfather's hand was a bunch of the long-stemmed dark red flowers of the Pitcher Plant (*Sarracenia purpurea*).
>
> These flowers came from "the bog" where Grandfather Fenwick had started in 1857 the culture of cranberries. Many were the treasures that came to that little granddaughter from "the bog": great mats of Pixie-moss (*Pyxidanthera barbulata*) thickly dotted with pink buds which opened into starry, white flowers;

154

spicy red Tea Berries (*Gaultheria procumbens*), a delight to the eye and so good to eat; a tiny turtle perhaps or a stem of Tiger Lilies (*Lilium superbum*).[148]

When the child turned ten, she lost her grandfather and her father, Joseph J. White, took charge. . . . It was his daughter's delight to share his plans and to associate with the lovely wild bog plants.[149]

A favorite of Elizabeth, and a rare plant of the bogs, was the Pine Barren Gentian (*Gentiana autumnalis*). She writes:

The day I first saw it is engraved in my memory as clearly as the day I first saw the Pitcher Plant flowers. . . . In the morning the bogs were too wet to pick and I was free for a few hours. So father and I, in the buggy behind plump, brown Daisy, started off to see how picking progressed with our neighbors a few miles away.

The winding, sandy road wandered through a stretch of low ground where water stood in the ruts. On the two parallel ridges between the wheel tracks and that worn by horses' hoofs were little hedges of all the native plants. . . . Like the whole country, these little hedges were glorious with the maroon, crimson, green and gold which autumn brings to the bog country of the Jersey Pines. . . . Suddenly amid the green of dwarf Laurel (*Kalmia angustifolia*)[150] and Sand Myrtle (*Leiophyllum buxifolium*) and the crimson of the Huckleberry (*Gaylussacia baccata*)[151] I spied a spot of bright blue. It was a gentian. We found five or six of them that morning. . . . The wide, open flowers were two inches and more in diameter, with five petals spreading out from the morning-glory-like throat, and a fringed septum joining the pointed petals for about a third of their length.[152]

Elizabeth was in her 50s before her famous garden became a reality. We have no record of such a garden at the family home in New Lisbon, where she lived from 1881–1924, but that does not preclude its existence or suggest that a hiatus occurred in her interest in native plants. One has only to peruse her early photographs to see the hold these wonders of nature had on her.

There are several pictures of Pitcher Plants, Grandfather Fenwick's gift; it also appears *Monotropa uniflora*, commonly known in the area as Indian Pipes, held a fascination for her.

Oral tradition has long held that Elizabeth White used the bequest left to her in her mother's will in 1923 as seed money to build a home at Whitesbog that she named Suningive. While the inheritance funds may have enabled actual construction to begin, a recent foray into the company minutes shows that plans for a Whitesbog home began before her mother's death, which occurred November 1, 1922. At the February 6, 1922, board meeting, a motion was introduced to build a house for Elizabeth at Whitesbog. The motion carried with the following stipulations: the building would serve first and foremost as her home. At the same time, it would provide Joseph J. White, Inc., with a company dispensary, a venue to entertain company guests, and a site for clerical work and other purposes.

In compensation for company use, J. J. White, Inc., would contribute $5,000 toward construction, as well as pay for insurance, repairs, and taxes. Elizabeth would be responsible for the remaining construction cost, funded with a 6 percent interest loan, and for ongoing costs to provide light, heat, provisions, and "help."

Elizabeth was not the first White daughter to consider a home at Whitesbog. Frank and Anne (White) Chambers cleared land for a home shortly after Frank began to work at the farm in 1911. They quickly abandoned plans due to Anne's health and the need for closer proximity to medical assistance.

Emlen and Mary (White) Darlington built a house at Whitesbog in 1914 and lived there for a year before returning to Fenwick Manor. Elizabeth was the only one to remain permanently in her own house at Whitesbog. The placement of the house had significance for her. Rimmed by pines, swamp cedars,[153] Red Maples, Gray Birches, Sour-Gums, and Swamp Magnolias, the ground on which Suningive was built had, for ten years, been one of the original blueberry test fields. A row of bushes, discarded for their fruit, but of lovely form and foliage, determined the exact location of the house which also overlooked one of Grandfather Fenwick's first cranberry bogs.[154] Around the area were also Swamp Azalea (*Rhododendron viscosum*), Aronia, or Red Chokeberry (*Aronia arbutifolia*), and Inkberry (*Ilex glabra*), all tangled with Greenbriar. As Miss White noted, "Good material this, but the effect was battered, bleak, unorganized."[155]

The main garden was not Elizabeth's first project. Grading was needed close to Suningive. Soil excavated from the blueberry patch left a hollow that she filled with water from a nearby irrigation ditch. With the water came lily seeds. By the second summer, there were green lily pads, and a year later glorious flowers. White was enamored of the beauty that surrounded her and she had the soul of a poet when describing it. Regarding the need for a yearly thinning out of the water lilies, she provides as a rationale, "to insure open water to mirror sunsets, the moon, and stars."[156]

Once the pond area itself was finished, Elizabeth began her primary landscaping project. As a foundation, she planted Mountain-laurel (*Kalmia latifolia*) and Inkberry (*Ilex glabra*), balancing their deep evergreen coloring with the lighter leafage of Red Chokeberry and Blueberry (*Vaccinium*). Like the blueberry bushes that formed the hedge around her home, the 'Grover #2' did not make the grade as a fruit producer, but it surpassed every other variety in the magnificence of its deep crimson coloring in autumn. Red Chokeberry offered two seasons of beauty. In spring, it put out flowers like tiny apple blossoms, while in fall, bright red berries graced the arched stems.

Elizabeth compared the work of a gardener to that of a sculptor, who shapes a lump of clay by adding some material here, removing some there, until a pleasing form emerges. Mats of Bearberry, already covering several areas closer to the house, were left in place for both beauty and usefulness.

> Its small, upright branches are covered with little leathery leaves, dark green in summer, red-brown in winter; in spring they are decked with tiny, inverted, pearly,

pink-tipped urns, and later red berries. The mats of Bearberry (*Arctostaphylos uva-ursi*) nurse many other plants of briefer beauty, such as the fall-flowering gold-enrods, purple and white asters, and purple wands of Liatris which open their flowers from the top down.[157]

Liatris may sound unfamiliar and exotic, but most people know it, thanks to the cut-flower industry. The long, purple spikes of *Liatris* often grace formal floral arrangements or may be included in a supermarket bouquet. This plant belongs to the aster family. Common names include Grass-leaf Blazing Star or Grassleaf Gayfeather. Witmer Stone called it Hairy Button Snakeroot (*Lacinaria graminifolia* var. *pilosa*), while other botanists referred to it as *Liatris graminifolia*. Today, it is known as *Liatris pilosa*. When the stalk begins to flower, the first buds appear at the top of the spike, which allows the top of the stalk to be cut off while the lower portion continues to bloom.

It would not be a Pine Barrens garden without moisture-loving plants, nor would it be Elizabeth White's garden without Pitcher Plants, Grandfather Fenwick's first gift from the bogs. She called sphagnum moss the "best nurse" for these additions to the landscape.

This was planted at the margins of the pool, sometimes in mats but often in little tufts four or five inches apart which soon covered the ground. Here are the Pitcher-plants. Some of the leaves, with their beautiful red veining, hold more than half a glass of rain water. In early summer, on stalks 18 inches high, these plants dangle flowers with big, floppy maroon petals. They drop soon after bees have brought pollen to the stigmas at the tips of the five ribs of a curious, inverted, central umbrella. The stems hold high the umbrella and glossy sepals until late fall, when the ripe seeds scatter.[158]

Pine Barrens orchids, another favorite, appeared abundantly around the pool. Elizabeth calls it a troop of Rose Pogonias (*Pogonia ophioglossoides*) and notes the single, pale pink, and delicately scented flower that topped each eight-inch stalk. This beauty was not isolated to the New Jersey bog lands. Robert Frost celebrated it in his first volume of poetry, *A Boy's Will*, published in 1915.

Rose Pogonias

A saturated meadow,
   Sun-shaped and jewel-small,
A circle scarcely wider
   Than the trees around were tall;
Where winds were quite excluded,
   And the air was stifling sweet
With the breath of many flowers,—
   A temple of the heat.

There we bowed us in the burning,
   As the sun's right worship is,
To pick where none could miss them
   A thousand orchises;
For though the grass was scattered,
   Yet every second spear

Seemed tipped with wings of color,
   That tinged the atmosphere.

We raised a simple prayer
   Before we left the spot,
That in the general mowing
   That place might be forgot;
Or if not all so favoured,
   Obtain such grace of hours,
That none should mow the grass there
   While so confused with flowers.[159]

One commentator calls Frost's offering a magical image, the description of a fairyland. White was an avid reader. Did she know of this poem? Did she read it? There are no volumes of Frost in what has been passed on as Elizabeth White's library, but the reverence for nature exhibited in Frost's work reflects that found in Elizabeth's own life and writings.

Two other Pine Barrens orchids found a home in the garden: Grass-pink (*Calopogon tuberosus*) and the White Fringed Orchid (*Platanthera blephariglottis*). These three graced the landscape from May into July, sharing their sphagnum-covered niche with three species of sundew. Each of the carnivorous plants was covered with red hairs, tipped with a sticky dew-like droplet to catch and, then, digest small insects. A collection of Venus Flytrap from North Carolina became a later addition to the garden. It is a bit surprising to hear the kind, big-hearted Elizabeth admit, "What fun to feed the leaves flies or tiny grasshoppers and see them quickly snap shut!"[160]

Elizabeth chose her plants with careful thought so that she would have blooms throughout the seasons. Summer must have provided a riot of colors for her enjoyment. Orange Milkwort (*Polygala lutea*) mingled with Gold-crest (*Lophiola aurea*), mats of Pyxie-moss, Pine Barren Gentian and Climbing-fern (*Lygodium palmatum*). Pyxie-moss and Sand-myrtle (*Leiophyllum buxifolium*) seem to have captured her descriptive imagination.

> The structure of this tiny shrub [Sand-myrtle] has, in miniature, all the picturesque rugged dignity of old rhododendrons. The small evergreen leaves have the same leathery quality. Starry white flowers smother the plants in May, but before the flowers open each little bush has its own individual bud color. Some are crimson, some pink, and others greenish white.[161]

> Perhaps the most loveable of all the Pine Barren plants is the Pyxie (*Pyxidanthera barbulata*),[162] frequently called Pyxie-moss or even Flowering Moss. It is really a woody shrub with evergreen leaves, but, unless struggling in the shade of larger shrubs, it grows no more than half an inch high. Its prostrate branches spread out on the surface of the ground. When young, the plants are green stars flat on the earth with five or more slender branches one to two inches long. As the plant grows older it forms a mat, for all the world like a patch of starry moss . . . Early in the spring each green star of the mossy surface develops in its center a pearly pink bud. These open into flat, five-peaked, white flowers, a quarter of an inch in diameter, each

just touching its neighbors, . . . When in full bloom and viewed from some distance Pyxie looks like a dropped white handkerchief.[163]

Elizabeth loved all her Pine Barrens plants, but she also invited guests into her garden, plants from other localities that could thrive in a Pine Barrens landscape. The introductions included Scotch Heather, Carolina Rhododendron, and the Venus Flytrap previously mentioned. She knew she had created something special; Suningive and the surrounding garden made a unified whole. The only thing missing was a lawn.

How lovely is a good lawn! But so difficult to maintain on the sand surrounding Suningive. The cranberry bog would serve as the lawn. It had been started by my grandfather, had furnished the means for Suningive, and inspiration for its garden. For 100 acres from the windows it stretches to the distant, dark, encircling rim of pines. Its velvety surface, green in summer, gradually turns to deep maroon by the middle of October. In December the bogs are flooded and, for garden purposes, lawn becomes lake—deep blue beneath clear skies; flashing with diamonds on sunny days; dark and glowering, with white caps racing before an easterly storm wind; smooth, still, and shining when Jack Frost lays his quieting hand upon it.[164]

Elizabeth wanted others to appreciate and love the beauty of the bog-lands as she did. As her grandfather and father had tutored her, she took the time introducing others to her magnificent world, if only they showed an interest. Elizabeth Kite was one of her pupils. Kite describes one of their sessions:

> Our objective that morning was "Buffin's Meadow," a great wilderness of untamed bog-land, and our car drew up when we touched its outmost rim.
>
> Stilled by an inner awe, as well as by the voice of my friend, I sank on a mossy bank, hands clasped in ecstasy, for before me, on a slight elevation, glittering in the sun's bright rays, was what seemed an innumerable company of tiny fairy folk suddenly stopped in a merry round danced to faint bog-land music. . . . What were they, this fairy folk, so dainty and so gay in the morning sun? Indeed, they were old friends, but never before had I seen them so numerous or so dazzling beautiful. For the instant, I seemed transported to a world as remote from the great city I had left as though I had landed upon some distant planet. In reality, these tiny folk were superb specimens of *Drosera filiformis*, or Sundew.[165]

While it gave Elizabeth joy to create new enthusiasts through personal, one-on-one instruction, it provided her with only a limited approach. Elizabeth seized opportunities as they presented themselves. In a letter to Chester M. Chaney of the American Cranberry Exchange, she expressed regret for having missed the August 1932 Annual Convention of the American Cranberry Growers Association. She explained her absence:

> The Flower Show in Atlantic City offered a rare opportunity to introduce to nurserymen a couple

of plants for which we were desirous of securing a wholesale outlet and when we were urged to put on a Wild Garden we accepted the chance. We believe we made good, but only time will tell.[166]

The Atlantic City show proved a three-pronged success. Elizabeth sought to educate nurserymen in Pine Barren plants and promote sales; a large audience had the pleasure of actually seeing the beauty of a garden like Elizabeth's; and Elizabeth and her nurseryman, Tom Windon, came home to Whitesbog with a medal.

Emerging technology offered Elizabeth another alternative. In the late 1870s, Heinrich Hertz discovered radio waves. Inventors vied to develop practical applications and, by 1910, these various wireless systems became known as "radio." Bamberger Broadcasting Service established WOR radio in 1922. Louis Bamberger owned a chain of department stores in New Jersey. He thought his employees could sell radios much more easily if the store operated its own radio studio, which he located on the sixth floor of the store's Newark headquarters. One of the more popular programs airing over WOR was the Radio Garden Club. Elizabeth White appeared on this show twice that can be substantiated. On June 6, 1937, she presented a recap of her blueberry experiences, and, in 1941, she spoke about her garden of Pine Barren plants. The transcript from this latter broadcast provided most of the plant descriptions identified above as filling her garden. Others come from articles written for the *Bulletin of the American Rock Garden Society* and *Wise-Acres*, a publication of the Pennsylvania School of Horticulture for Women.

Blueberries

In concluding her radio presentation of the blueberry adventure, Miss White urged the listeners to consider introducing blueberry plants into their gardens for their ornamental beauty, as well as for their fruit. She eloquently voiced their allure throughout the year:

> Every season brings special and unusual beauty. In spring, the dainty foliage and great clusters of snowy white flower bells, suggesting those of the Lily-of-the-valley, unfold at the same time. Many varieties have crimson tipped flower buds. Summer beauty reaches its peak when the clusters of fruit are ripening "just like grapes," as nearly every visitor says. The laden bushes are glamorous with fruit showing lovely cool tones of frosted green, pink and blue against the deep green foliage. Autumn brings to none of our trees or bushes more brilliant reds than to blueberries, and when hard freezing takes away the fullest blaze of the foliage, the color does not fade to ashen gray, for the bark of the twigs is bright all winter. Seen from upper windows during December, January, February and well into March, blueberry fields are marvels of beauty, acres of soft deep crimson against a background of dark green pines and tawny oaks still holding persistently their brown leaves. A blueberry hedge near my office window is a joy all winter long. Its red twigs catch and hold myriads of raindrops, pearly under cloudy skies. Again, the red branches gleam warmly through sleety armor, or uphold feathery fluffs of snow.[167]

Holly

Holly propagation provided another one of Elizabeth's fascinations. The establishment of Holly Haven in the 1950s could suggest her interest developed late in life after blueberries had become a fixture in the horticultural community. However, this was not so. J. J. White owned much property in the town of New Lisbon, where the family lived. Bob Reeves, a New Lisbon resident, a fellow blueberry farmer, and a member of Grace Episcopal Church where Miss White also worshiped, remembers Elizabeth's using the land on Meadow View Lane as a holly nursery until the field underwent subdivision and was sold off as individual plots. She grew holly trees at Whitesbog as well. Recorded in the Joseph J. White, Inc., ledgers are conservation nursery sales in the 1920s that include some holly along with blueberry bushes, Franklinia trees, and native plants.

At this time, buyers showed no eagerness in purchasing hollies. Many thought the plants proved difficult to transplant; seedlings took eight to ten years to fruit. Since the plant had distinct sexes, placing males and females in the right proximity to insure fruiting could be complex. Many northern gardeners did not think holly was sufficiently hardy. Individuals like Elizabeth White took up the challenge to remove these barriers, one by one. In a 1941 interview with Charles P. Shoffner,[168] moderator of the farm and garden report for WCAU radio in Philadelphia, Elizabeth described her goal in working with holly as stopping the devastation of native stands. She hoped to accomplish this objective by "providing holly plants so good that gardeners can easily grow and enjoy this most beautiful of Christmas trees."[169]

In the short time it took to answer eight straight-forward questions, White imparted a good deal of knowledge about hollies. When questioned about the berries, she informed her audience that, usually, holly plants are either male or female, that only female plants bear berries, and that until the trees bloom and produce berries, it is impossible to tell the boys from the girls. If the holly were to be raised from seed, this process would take a long time, since the seeds usually take two years to germinate, followed by five or six years of growth before any berries appear. Elizabeth also stated that she preferred working with cuttings because she found seedlings unreliable in producing consistent quality. She had learned this lesson well through her blueberry experimentation. Also, as with the blue-berry experience, her holly specimens all came from the wild, even though some had spent many years on the grounds of old New Jersey homesteads being protected. Although some of the trees taken directly from the wild may have appeared of lower quality than those cared for so well, when placed side by side in the nursery, the innate quality of the plant itself showed forth.

Shoffner questioned White about the differences in hollies. Elizabeth cited size, leaf quality, and berry production as examples. Some hollies grow to be tall trees; others remain bush size. In the open fields, rows of some plants burn and turn brown under winter winds, while having no effect on the leaves of trees in the adjoining rows. Some female plants produce copious amounts of berries regularly, while others produce scantily or irregularly. Berries may be red or scarlet or yellow, small or large, round or oval. Elizabeth White's appearance on WCAU paralleled one George Nearing, another holly enthusiast, made three years earlier. On December 8, 1938, he used his appearance on a WOR broadcast to encourage Garden Club listeners to select, name, and propagate American hollies to keep them from extinction. Each of them addressed a different audience; Philadelphia and its suburbs heard White, while Nearing reached New Jersey and New York listeners.

By the time Elizabeth White sat for the interview with Shoffner, she had studied holly for about fifteen years on her own and three years in conjunction with Wilfrid Wheeler, a skilled Massachusetts horticulturist who, like Elizabeth, had enthusiastically sought out local stands of holly to evaluate them for eventual commercial propagation. Wheeler had a long and stellar history in Massachusetts agriculture. In 1919, the governor appointed him as the state's first commissioner of agriculture. Prior to that time, he served as secretary for the old State Board of Agriculture. In 1925, Wilfred Wheeler bought about 300 acres of land, mainly in Hatchville (now a neighborhood in northern Falmouth) and Mashpee, which he called Ashumet Farm and where he started his holly program. What began as a professional exchange between two horticultural conservationists, developed into mutual respect and a friendship that spanned three decades and more than 100 letters. Wheeler initiated their "conversations" on November 10, 1938:

My dear Miss White;

I have heard through a friend of mine that you are collecting the various types of *Ilex opaca* in your section; this has been a hobby of mine for quite a while and I have several that vary a great deal from each other. You probably have the same variation, but if it would be of any interest to you I will send you some fruit of the samples that I have to compare with yours. I am trying to propagate the best types and have several of these under cultivation.[170]

Four days later, Elizabeth replied:

My dear Mr. Wheeler:

I am very much interested to learn from your letter of November 10 of your work with holly. It would interest me to see the fruit, as you suggest, though I find the quality of the leaves and the general type of the plant are quite as much interest as the berries . . . Because of the difficulty in protecting outstanding wild trees, I feel that the selection and propagation of holly, such as you are doing and I am doing, is one of the finest contributions to conservation.[171]

In that introductory exchange, Wheeler also spoke of his interest in other species of holly such as *Ilex aquifolium* (English holly), *I. vomitoria* (yaupon holly or Appalachian tea), *I. cornuta* (Chinese holly) and *I. latifolia* (lusterleaf holly). This mirrors people's interest in holly through the ages. Plants in the holly family have been widely used in landscaping and in holiday decorations. Because English holly keeps its dark green leaves and bears bright red fruit in the wintertime, it served for centuries as a symbol of Christmas and other winter celebrations. European immigrants to North America continued the tradition by using American holly in the same way. Elizabeth preferred to stay with American holly (*Ilex opaca*) and told this to Wheeler. White concludes her letter with the news that she has taken a break in her work and at the moment has no holly of considerable size. A search in the Joseph J. White, Inc., ledgers revealed the reason for this hiatus. The sash house,[172] used for holly propagation, suffered partial destruction from fire in October 1936. The company carried no insurance on that building, which delayed reconstruction.

After the first letter, it appeared that both Wheeler and White were eager to get down to business sharing information and experiences. The two shipped plant samples back and forth. Each offered honest opinions on the samples sent. In January 1939, Wilfrid Wheeler had sent Elizabeth White three cuttings from three different holly trees. After receiving and examining the shipment, Elizabeth wrote back, "I should say your No. 3 is not worth bothering with. The foliage is poor, and the berries are of too dark red for the color to carry. No. 1 and No. 2, however, seem to me to be rarely beautiful, with good foliage and heavy fruiting of very large, bright scarlet berries."[173]

They also exchanged selections that they had named. Elizabeth dispatch samples of 'Osa,' 'Clark,' 'Manig,' 'Laura,' 'Joyce' and 'Griscom,' "the best of New Jersey," to Massachusetts and, in return, Whitesbog received some of Wheeler's best like 'Emily,' 'Dorothy,'

'Wilson,' 'St Mary' and 'Aalto.' Wheeler and White helped each other in practical ways as well. They often bought stock from each other to replenish quantity and variety in their respective nurseries. Elizabeth's account of the number of cuttings in her nursery is reminiscent of her blueberry experiment days. In November 1941, she writes, "To the best of my knowledge and belief, we have the only supply of selected northern hollies."[174]

One of the major contributions that these two conservationists gave to the field of holly study was the selection of varieties of *I. opaca*, taken both from the wild and local residential sites, for propagation and commercialization. They corresponded about the merits of particular plants, and, on occasion, went on plant hunting expeditions together, although the gas rationing of the war years made such trips infrequent occurrences. After one trip, Elizabeth wrote, asking, "Are you expecting to send cuttings of the other two trees we located in the woods? They were near the Girl Scouts' camp, were they not?"[175] The following year, Wheeler acknowledged that scouting expeditions wore him out and he could no longer indulge in such pleasures on a regular basis.

Appendix C shows the specific holly plants attributed to Elizabeth White, both individually and in collaboration with Wilfrid Wheeler and Thomas Windon. Hired in 1923 as the primary blueberry propagationist, Windon became interested in holly as well; perhaps Miss White persuaded him. Blueberry bushes remained big business, but, as Elizabeth complained to Wheeler, none of her associates but Windon showed any interest in hollies. Together, Elizabeth and Tom scoured the area around Whitesbog in search of suitable stock. They made cuttings, which they passed on to Windon's twin daughters for planting.

The folks at Whitesbog, if that is whom Elizabeth was referring to as her associates, may not have been holly enthusiasts, but there were others in New Jersey and the Northeast who were. In their letters, both Mr. Wheeler and Elizabeth White frequently commented on the views and accomplishments of other holly aficionados. The most prominent holly fans in New Jersey included Clarence R. Wolf and Daniel Fenton of Millville; George G. Nearing, who moved his nurseries from Delaware to Ridgewood, New Jersey, after World War II; and Earle Dilatush, whose had a holly nursery in Robbinsville.

Beginning in 1926, Wolf, the President of New Jersey Silica Sand Company, gave holly as a Christmas gift to his customers from the trees growing on his company property. The gifts were appreciated and, year after year, people requested holly boughs to decorate their homes for Christmas. Wolf wanted to insure sufficient holly to continue his Christmas custom, and so, in 1939, he established a 68-acre farm consisting of superior native trees selected from the wild and trees taken from Silica Sand property. Under the direction of Daniel Fenton, it was, at one time, the largest American holly orchard in the United States.

In 1936, Jackson (Jack) Batchelor, horticulturist with the USDA, met Wilfrid Wheeler at Ashumet Farm. Bachelor had come to Massachusetts looking for beach plums; it did not take Wheeler long to interest him in holly. For his part, Batchelor encouraged a holly curiosity in Harry Dengler, Extension Forester at Maryland University, whom he met in the early 1940s.

In 1944, Batchelor and Dengler attended a meeting at Eastern Shore, Maryland, where they met Elizabeth White and Earle Dilatush. These two convinced Dengler to devote his energies to American holly and, with Batchelor, urged him to form a Maryland holly society. While Dengler busied himself with promoting the case for holly in Maryland, similar efforts were taking place in New Jersey. Charles H. Connors initiated a holly research program at the College of Agriculture, Rutgers University. Connors and two members of the Agriculture Extension Service, along with Elizabeth White, Wilfrid Wheeler, and G. G. Nearing, received an invitation to the home of Judge Thomas Brown to view a large collection of excellent native American holly. Unfortunately, Wheeler could not attend. With their mutual interest in American holly, the New Jersey Holly Research Committee formed. Judge Brown was named chairman and Charles Connors, vice-chairman.

On April 18, 1947, Harry Dengler called a meeting of the Maryland Holly Society. He invited the newly formed Holly Research Committee of New Jersey and Clarence Wolf. The formation of a national association was discussed, and a motion passed to combine the Maryland and New Jersey groups into the Holly Society of America.[176] Those present nominated a board of trustees, but no vote occurred at that first session. Clarence Wolf was tentatively nominated as President, Harry Dengler as Vice-President, and Mr. and Mrs. Charles A. Young,[177] Secretary-treasurer. They decided to add a fifth trustee and selected Daniel Fenton of Millville.

On June 24, 1947, the five trustees met at Wolf's office in Millville, New Jersey, where they crafted, approved and signed the incorporation document and by-laws of the Holly Society of America (HSA). The organizers made plans for the first official meeting, to be held in November 1947, again in Millville, the Holly Capital of America. Elizabeth C. White and June Vail became charter members of the Society, as did Wilfrid Wheeler. In recognition of their many contributions to the study and conservation of holly, on April 9, 1954, during the annual meeting, the HSA presented Wheeler and White its Distinguished Members Award, a stained-glass plaque with holly motif, which Forrest Crooks, an artisan from Doylestown, Pennsylvania, created.

Penn Trees

In 1932, the city of Philadelphia celebrated the 250th anniversary of William Penn's founding of Pennsylvania, "Penn's Woods," in a grand way. Charles F. Jenkins served as Executive Chairman for the William Penn Commemoration. As part of the extravaganza, Edward E. Wildman, of the Philadelphia school system, conceived the idea to identify and register trees still extant in Pennsylvania, New Jersey, Delaware, and the eastern shore of Maryland, from the time of Penn's first visit to the region in 1682. The search resulted in a tree survey book published in 1933; Jenkins wrote the Introduction to Wildman's book.

Elizabeth White was listed as one of the New Jersey locators of a Penn tree, but this section of the book did not always link the locators and their identified trees. There are two possibilities for Elizabeth's find, however, based on location:

> Going east to Pemberton and north about two miles on the Arney' Mount Road one sees a pin oak on the west side of the highway. . . . A mile farther north beside the picturesque old Meeting House at Arney's Mount stands a white oak of great age.[178]

Pemberton Borough is adjacent to Pemberton Township. The latter includes Browns Mills and Whitesbog. Arney's Mount, Springfield Township, features the Quaker Meeting that J. J. White attended. Of all the New Jersey trees mentioned, these two are most logically connected to the Whites.

Wildman went out to his original tree finders a second time about eight years later. In 1940, he requested an update on each tree in connection with a study of the climatic conditions in the Delaware Valley and their influence on tree growth. Wildman provided very specific instructions for measuring increase in growth and gathering specimens in case the tree no longer stood. Wildman added a handwritten note to Elizabeth's letter, making an additional request, not associated with her nomination or even a Penn tree. Wildman expressed special interest in old white cedar and knew that the trees thrived in a locale like the Pine Barrens. He hoped to be able to receive a cross-section of an "old white cedar of known date at the bark." Elizabeth took the time to try to honor this request. She paid a visit to Mr. Mick, a mill man, and learned that he was in the process of clearing a cedar swamp and could provide the cross-sections. Wildman received the cuttings he required and a word of caution for his analysis. Sharing her knowledge of pine barrens plants, Elizabeth wrote:

> In judging the weather conditions from the width of the rings of white cedar I would suggest that you take into consideration the fact that poor drainage in a cedar swamp inhibits the growth of the tree. Therefore, in the case of this particular tree, the narrower rings may indicate a particularly wet season rather than a particularly dry season.[179]

There is one last association with Penn trees. On May 25, 1951, the Penn Treaty Committee of Bowman's Hill Wild Flower Preserve in Washington Crossing Park dedicated a scion of the Penn Treaty Elm in honor of Miss Elizabeth C. White.

Elizabeth C. White: A Life Well Lived
A Life in Balance

A strong work ethic guided the Fenwick and White families. Growing up in this atmosphere, Elizabeth White both absorbed and retained this philosophy, but it represented just one side of the coin. She was also taught that all things in life had to be kept in balance. There was a time for work and just as importantly, a time for play. We have seen Elizabeth at work; now it is time to see her at play.

"Play" means different things to different people. For some, it means physical or outdoor activities like hiking or boating. For others, play is watching a movie, or going to a play, or even reading a good book. And for some, just getting together with friends is a source of enjoyable relaxation. Elizabeth re-energized her spirit through all these and more. Photography may well have topped the list of Elizabeth's sources of recreation. No available documentation mentions when or how this interest began or how she developed her expertise. It has been a supposition at Whitesbog that Elizabeth took classes in photography at Drexel Institute. As mentioned earlier, when discussing her education, while possible, this theory is probably unlikely. What it does suggest is that she had an interest in the art when she graduated from high school. With the introduction and growing popularity of gelatin dry plates around 1880, followed by roll film in 1888, amateur photography began to spread rapidly. Some novice camera buffs gained satisfaction and personal enjoyment through self-experimentation; others sought to expand their expertise through more formal education and sharing their work with experts for professional critique.

Both could be accomplished by joining a photographic society. The first such institution in New Jersey would not be established until 1935 in Princeton, but Elizabeth would have had an opportunity much earlier. The Photographic Society of Philadelphia, the oldest in the country, was founded in 1860. If she aligned herself with this group, she would have had a support group for encouragement and improvement in her technique. There is a group of photos in Whitesbog's archives that could have populated either an educational or exhibition portfolio. More than likely, it was the latter, as the type of photographic prints appears to be of a more advanced technology than some of her other work.

We cannot discount Elizabeth's self-instruction through reading. At some point, she subscribed to *The American Amateur Photographer*. In addition to informative articles on current trends in photography, the publishers offered to critique their readers' work and, as a regular feature each month, published their opinion of selected entries.[180] Elizabeth took advantage of the opportunity on at least two occasions. Her first submission selected for review appeared in the December 1898 issue.

The number the periodical assigned to her entry was an innovation introduced earlier that year as a reference mechanism. It allowed a reader to identify the photo, when appearing in a subsequent issue, and then to go back and consult the original critique.

> 222. Elizabeth C. White. "Wildflowers" is a very fine subject photographed from the very worst point of view. It is "a path through the wood where wildflowers grow" but photographed from the middle, so that the path instead of running out, goes straight from the middle of the foreground up to the center of the horizon; and to make the composition still more mechanical, one of the two fair flower-gatherers is placed on each side of the path. If cut vertically in two, each half would be as like to the other as two peas, which is fatal to pictorial effect. It should have been photographed from far enough to the right or left to make the path go out of the picture. It is also very much under-exposed, so that the tree trunks are simply black paper and the faces that should be and doubtless are fair, are of African darkness. With all its faults, however, it shows that when our correspondent has given the necessary study to composition and realized that such subjects cannot be taken with snaps or short exposures, she will be a credit to the craft.[181]

Elizabeth's second critique followed quickly; she probably submitted the two pictures together. This time, her photograph of a mother duck and ducklings was analyzed (the photograph survives in the Whitesbog archives; see a reproduction on p. 203). In the January 1899 issue, the following appeared:

241. Elizabeth C. White. "Their First Appearance," a duck with ducklings just hatched is a very good photograph and a proof that you are quite able to tackle more interesting subjects. We shall reproduce it as an example of perfect technique.[182]

The photo appeared a few months later in the June issue.

From the two examples noted above, we can surmise that Elizabeth rooted much of her photography in nature. Family and close friends also found their way into her repertoire. Being an organized person, she maintained a photo log, including the date taken, at least for the early images. From this list can be learned what subjects interested her. Between March 1896 and October 1901, she cataloged 300 pictures. Compared to the total collection, however, only a small portion has found its way into the Whitesbog archives. If Elizabeth maintained the practice of cataloging her collection beyond 1901, Whitesbog's loss is even greater. What the archives holds stands as a testament to Elizabeth's artistic soul: whimsical studies of nesting geese and gosling, a playful shot of her sister Beulah and the family dog, Don;[183] delicate images of a spider's web; and a spray of blueberry blossoms. Bucolic settings pay tribute to the beauty found in her family's agricultural background. A peaceful field studded with haystacks; a huge sprawling oak; cattle drinking at Halstead Pond; and the tree-lined road leading up to her father's ancestral home, SHARON, all speak to her pride in her heritage. Elizabeth's photographs also reflect the closeness among the members of the extended White family: her cousins Rebecca Shrigley, Mary Bartram and her husband Harry, and Howard White, Mary's brother, often appear in her snapshots.[184]

The pictures that have not survived also tell a story. Her list shows that she frequently photographed people. Outside of the handful of group photos in which her sisters, together with cousins or friends, appear, however, these images are curiously absent in the collection that has endured. It may be that her heirs shared the photographs with the subjects after Elizabeth died. Some are of family, friends, and employees with whom she was in frequent contact and whose relationship is documented elsewhere, as in Beulah's diary. Other missing photographs depict individuals known through a connection in the cranberry industry. Why these individuals? Were they also frequent visitors at Fenwick Manor and just not mentioned elsewhere? If Elizabeth had kept a diary—she did not—each of these folks would be more familiar, for they certainly held enough importance for her to want to have a reminder of them.

From some other photos noted in her catalog, Elizabeth seemed to enjoy people-watching. Each year, she had a wonderful opportunity to observe the tourists who summered in New Lisbon. Several entries chronicle this activity. "New Lisbon boarders on porch, boating, and bathing" were three. Elizabeth must have often gone out with no special target in mind, assured that something intriguing would present itself. Catching a gentleman named Paul half asleep was just one example. Where was Paul and what was he supposed to be doing? We'll never know. Coming upon Kittie Silverheels while baking cookies provided a glimpse of another ordinary everyday experience. One glaring absence in Elizabeth's list is her Uncle Dan, Aunt Serena, and Atlantic City, considering the frequency with which she, as well as the entire family, visited. Daniel Smith White built the famous Traymore Hotel in that city and he often entertained family members there. Besides Atlantic City, the White girls also visited other Jersey shore resorts. Elizabeth's catalog mentions outings to Asbury Park and Seaside Park, although no photos survive from these locations.

Travel provided Elizabeth with a wealth of material for her growing portfolio. Regrettably, the only prints remaining from this category are those taken during a family trip to the Mediterranean and Egypt. In 1904, Uncle Dan White and his wife Serena invited Elizabeth and Mary to accompany the couple on this exciting journey. Cousin Josiah White, his wife Mary, and daughters Frances and Gertrude rounded out the travel partners.

It may be apropos, at this point, to offer a little background on Daniel and Josiah White. As mentioned previously, Daniel White was J. J. White's half-brother, the son of Barclay and Beulah Shreve White. Like the other White brothers, Daniel was an enterprising person. In 1879, he opened a small boarding house in Atlantic City which, after suffering a destructive fire, underwent reconstruction and burgeoned into the sumptuous Traymore Hotel. Across from the Traymore stood the equally famed Marlborough-Blenheim, built by Josiah White, a cousin to J. J. and Daniel. In 1904, at the time of the trip, Josiah was proprietor of the more modest, but quite successful, Marlborough

House, while construction of the new, expanded hotel continued.[185]

The group embarked on the Express-Steamer AUGUST VICTORIA on February 2, 1904, the time of year most cranberry growers found it convenient to travel. The 1903 harvest proved heavy, with a little over 27,000 bushels picked. Both White daughters had participated, Elizabeth overseeing the picking and Mary supervising the sorting. The intervening ocean voyage allowed the sisters to rest before undertaking the exploration that lay ahead. The profusion of photographs taken on the trip makes it very clear that the next two months comprised a whirlwind of movement and sightseeing. History must have come alive as the tourists visited the Pyramids, old Memphis, Syracuse, Pompeii, and the Alhambra. Strange cultures expanded their horizons in Jerusalem and its environs. Both the people and their bucolic way of life found their way into Elizabeth's photo album. From Asia Minor, the travelers moved to Italy. Based on the number of photographs exposed here, it appears Elizabeth took a special interest in the churches and other examples of medieval architecture. From Italy, the weary, but contented, entourage made its way home. Snapshots show happy vacationers, relaxing on the return voyage, probably savoring and recounting their favorite memories.

Five years later, Elizabeth again traveled abroad, this time in the company of her sister Beulah. The young women spent four months on a glorious adventure. Thanks to Beulah's diary, a record exists of the comprehensive, yet arduous, trip. Elizabeth kept her memories through her photographs, which again, are either lost or in another's custody. On March 25, 1909, the sisters boarded the COLONIAL EXPRESS, traveling to Boston to await passage. Two days later, they met up with the rest of their tour group and set sail on the White Star liner CANOPIE. During the five-day ocean voyage, the group passed the time attending lectures their tour leader offered about the places and sights they would see. Finally, on April 2, the ship docked in Porta Del Garda in the Azores. After a quick one-day excursion to Gibraltar and Algiers, the group moved on to Italy, where they spent a full month. They visited all the major cities and tourist spots like Naples, Rome, Venice, Florence, Milan, and Pisa, as well as some smaller sites like Padua, Brindisi, and Assisi; time even permitted a side trip to Mt. Etna in Sicily. The time in Italy was divided in two with a three-week trip to Greece. The travelers immersed themselves in the history of Athens, Sparta, Thermopylae, and Marathon.

Leaving from Milan, the group moved on to the rest of Europe, which they investigated at a more rapid pace as the itinerary allowed only three days each in Switzerland, Germany, and Holland. Only a few places in each country made the list: Berne, Cologne, and Amsterdam among them. From the Netherlands, the group headed to the English and Scottish countryside. A week in London and a week in Paris rounded out the trip. The weary tourists had a short rest in Antwerp before boarding the ZEELAND for the journey home on July 18, 1909. The ocean voyage proved long, so when the ship docked in New York on July 28, Elizabeth and Beulah were both happy and grateful to see a welcome party waiting for them. J. J., Frank, Mary, and friends, the Clevengers, shepherded the young women to the train that would take them to their overnight lodging in Philadelphia.

The following morning, they traveled by ferry to Camden, where they took a train that would finally bring them home to New Lisbon. The young women had been gone for four months. The cranberry harvest was just a month away. The girls were not ready to settle into a business mode just yet, but they desired to share all their wonderful memories with family and friends. What better way to do this than through Elizabeth's photos? Beulah willingly helped to make prints to take to Aunt Serena and Uncle Dan in Atlantic City. Regrettably, the images are not available in the archives to share the experience. If someone has been entrusted with what must have been a wonderful collection, it is not the Whitesbog Preservation Trust.

Elizabeth White often traveled to fill speaking requests, attend meetings, and seek out plant specimens like holly. No documentation in publicly available sources exists to determine whether she ever took another vacation on the scale of the two overseas adventures just described, although June Vail suggests Elizabeth visited Yellowstone and the Grand Canyon. If so, she would have stood in awe at landscapes so different from her own. Elizabeth did enjoy visiting Atlantic City and the Poconos, despite not being exotic destinations. Beulah's diary features frequent entries describing visits to Uncle Dan and Aunt Serena at the Jersey Shore. Sometimes the outing included horseback riding on the beach, an activity allowed at the time. Both Elizabeth and Beulah enjoyed riding and often did it together at home. June Vail remembered that Elizabeth took her personal horse with her on trips to the Poconos, where one of her cousins managed the Skytop Resort. Asbury Park was also a shore destination for picnics and photo ops.

What other interests did Elizabeth pursue in her free time? As often as possible, she took advantage of New Lisbon's proximity to Philadelphia, with its many offerings of cultural events. Along with the rest of the family, Elizabeth attended plays, operas, and lectures. Music was also a staple in the White household. Beulah and Anne played the organ at church services; Beulah gave piano lessons; J. J. brought home a phonograph player shortly after it came onto the market. It is unknown whether Elizabeth played an instrument, but she most surely would have had an appreciation of music. Cultural opportunities also occurred closer to home. Beulah White's diary mentions Sunday evening lectures in New Lisbon in a way that suggests they happened frequently.

What did Elizabeth do on those days when she just wanted a little down-time at home? Perhaps she indulged her fancy and created a new hat or a new outfit. She also would be happy for a chance to sit quietly and read. The books she has left behind include topics like biography, horticulture, and history, while her magazine selections appear limited to popular gardening publications. Her expense account indicates she subscribed to the Book-of-the-Month Club. Lastly, we cannot forget the USDA bulletins and other scientific reports so important in keeping abreast of the ever-changing agricultural environment.

As strange as it may seem, Elizabeth's willingness to accept so many invitations to lecture on and exhibit her blueberry experience appears to indicate that the sharing provided its own source of energy and strength. Between exerting the drive that resulted in her excelling in all her duties at Whitesbog, and having so many choices to sustain her spirit, Elizabeth surely often wished for more hours in the day.

Sadly, the time arrived when Elizabeth's strength simply ran out. In 1945, she suffered a stroke, but fought her way back to reasonable health. The founding of Holly Haven provided the type of challenge that energized her, and offered her a new career. This time, however, motivation was not enough. Elizabeth's body succumbed to her battle with cancer. She died in her home, Suningive, on November 27, 1954. Whitesbog had been Elizabeth's life for more than sixty years. She would not leave it in death. In accordance with the stipulation in her will, her body was cremated and her ashes scattered over the headwaters at Whitesbog.

Epilogue

Up to this point, we have observed Elizabeth White in action. We have seen what Elizabeth accomplished. All the successes and failures emanated from Elizabeth's essence, but just who was Elizabeth Coleman White?

She proved to be a complex, multi-faceted woman. Her variable interests and skills might be likened to the ever-changing refractions of a kaleidoscope, presenting different and fascinating patterns with each rotation of the tube. Let us view Elizabeth as her inner self is reflected through the mirrors of her life.

Our first view shows Elizabeth as a family member. She is fiercely loyal and her pride in them echoes loud and strong through her recounting of family accomplishments in her many speeches and addresses. She was especially devoted to her father. In December 1923, the Wisconsin cranberry growers asked Elizabeth to address them at an upcoming meeting. She declined, citing her father's illness as the reason.

> The acute illness of last summer partially deprived my father of the understanding and use of words, either spoken or on paper, and he is still feeble. He takes such pleasure in the comradeship established by our years of work together and is so cut off from other interests that at present I am unwilling to leave home even for a few days.[186]

Let's turn the kaleidoscope to see Elizabeth within the cranberry grower community, which, aside from her family and a few close friends, was the longest continuous relationship of her life. Her initiation into this group was marked with humility and patience as she waited close to twenty years for formal inclusion through membership. She used the opportunity to demonstrate her willingness to learn and to participate in every aspect of cranberry culture, even unassuming tasks like collecting insects for entomologist John Smith's studies. Under the guidance of her father and the other growers, Elizabeth not only grew in confidence as a knowledgeable cranberry woman, but also inspired the other growers to trust her abilities.

When the National Child Labor Committee issued its accusations, the Cranberry Growers Association first turned to Joseph J. White to respond on their behalf. Once he became ill and unable to continue in this role, the Association turned to Elizabeth. They knew they could depend on her and felt secure as she championed their cause. Many would link Elizabeth's characteristic of forward-thinking with her blueberry endeavors. It also manifested itself in her cranberry work. In 1929, she made two impassioned speeches to the growers about the importance of continually improving the varieties of berries, and, being a "doer," she offered to experiment for them if they provided her with promising vines.

Another trait that we frequently associate with blueberry experimentation, but is also seen in her cranberry work, is that of a risk taker. People who are forward thinkers are often required to be risk takers. As the shift in berry use moved from fresh to processed fruit, Elizabeth joined the small group of cranberry farmers who saw the advantage of merging the two separate marketing agencies into one. She had to take a stand in opposition to those who preferred the *status quo*. Her own family stood among the latter. These same qualities, at times, exhibited themselves in a negative way. Some of Elizabeth's remarks pointed to impatience with those who could not see when the time had arrived to let go of the old ways. She was also critical when the members of the American Cranberry Exchange did not acknowledge and thank Marcus Urann for saving most of them from financial disaster in 1937.

What colorful array strikes our eyes if we turn our kaleidoscope into the blueberry arena? We see a decisive, determined, organized, energetic, and persevering woman. Here is an individual whose self-esteem has been nurtured to the point of being confident in her own abilities, yet cognizant of her own shortcomings. She is not afraid to admit what she does not know and to learn from those who do, like Frederick Coville. Elizabeth was quick to recognize and praise the contribution of others: Coville, the "Pineys" who found the bushes, Sidney Hutton who instigated the use of cellophane covering, or Ezekiel Sooy, whose blueberry bush, 'Sooy #1,' started the hybrid ball rolling.

Sharing the knowledge and encouraging new blueberry growers provided her with great joy. All her catalogs contained the information needed to grow blueberry bushes, whether for profit or for pleasure.

One last turn of the kaleidoscope shows Elizabeth within the community. Let's look first at the geographic communities of New Lisbon and Whitesbog. Her kindness extended itself to the local folks on many occasions. Her sister Beulah makes references to Elizabeth's taking ill neighbors to the hospital, to her attending women in childbirth, and to her pursuing medical care in Philadelphia for a lame child. In the last instance, when the doctors could do nothing, Elizabeth felt she had to do something and resorted to buying special shoes for the lad. This interest in and care for her neighbors was a trait that had been instilled in her from her earliest years. Her cultivation of it was yet another tribute to her family.

Once again relying on Beulah White's diary for family anecdotes, we discover that Elizabeth offered to care for Ethel and Birdsall Hornor, when their mother, Etta, was called away on a family emergency. Since the children's father was farm superintendent, Ivins Hornor, the offer was pragmatic as well as generous. Also, this probably ended up being a family project, not just Elizabeth's.

"Always feeling an interest in social work and uplift movements"[187] was how Elizabeth described herself to members of the representatives of the New Jersey Department of Charities and Corrections in Asbury Park. She was unwavering in her professed interest, backing up words with actions. For over twenty years (1910–1930), she pursued decent worker housing, first in her own farming community and, then, across the country through Hoover's housing study and recommendations. She was dogged and sometimes downright "pushy" in her efforts to improve rural education. Her enduring involvement in Four Mile Colony, and its subsequent evolutions, are testimony to her tenacity in this entire arena.

There is an old adage, "Put your money where your mouth is." Elizabeth did. In an old ledger, there is a record of Elizabeth White's personal accounts spanning 1940–1946. Although this is a relatively short period, the documented expenditures reflect her priorities. There were the usual household expenses: fees like insurance, memberships, and the like. Then there was consistent and generous support for Grace Episcopal Church. Allocations for personal items were few, but each month there were substantial donations. The recipients were almost always institutions of learning or organizations serving children.

Balance and inner calm describe the true nature of Elizabeth Coleman White, a woman ahead of her time and, yet, just right for her time. A woman just right for this time.

The White Family &
Elizabeth's Photographs

"Minnie" and "J. J." – Mary Anne Fenwick and Joseph Josiah White. *Courtesy of the Whitesbog Preservation Trust.*

Graduates of Friends Central School, 1890. Elizabeth is in the second row, third from the left. *Courtesy of Friends Central School.*

The Sharon homestead. *Courtesy of the Whitesbog Preservation Trust.*

The White sisters and cousins. (Left to right) Anne, Beulah, Rebecca Shrigley (cousin), Mary, Elizabeth, Mary Bartram (cousin). *Courtesy of the Whitesbog Preservation Trust.*

The White family. (Left to right) Beulah, Mary Anne Fenwick White, Anne (standing), Joseph Josiah White, Elizabeth, Mary, Grandmother Mary E. Cashell Fenwick. *Courtesy of the Whitesbog Preservation Trust.*

The White Cousins, June 12, 1897. (Left to right) Howard White Jr., Beulah White, Mary Bartram, Harry Bartram, Mary White, Rebecca Shrigley, and Anne Chambers. *Courtesy of Friends of Pemberton Library.*

Photograph by Elizabeth C. White. Submitted to *The American Amateur Photographer* and critiqued in the January 1899 issue; the photo appeared in the June 1899 issue. *Courtesy of the Whitesbog Preservation Trust.*

Photograph by Elizabeth C. White. Documenting blueberry development. *Courtesy of the Whitesbog Preservation Trust.*

Photograph by Elizabeth C. White. Cattle drinking at Halstead Pond. *Courtesy of the Whitesbog Preservation Trust.*

Photograph by Elizabeth C. White. *Monotropa uniflora*, commonly known in the area as Indian Pipes. *Courtesy of the Whitesbog Preservation Trust.*

Photograph by Elizabeth C. White. Cranberry bog. *Courtesy of the Whitesbog Preservation Trust.*

Photograph by Elizabeth C. White. European tour, 1909. *Courtesy of the Whitesbog Preservation Trust.*

Photograph by Elizabeth C. White. Elizabeth's sister Beulah and the family dog, Don. *Courtesy of the Whitesbog Preservation Trust.*

Photograph by Elizabeth C. White. At the spring. *Courtesy of the Whitesbog Preservation Trust.*

Elizabeth C. White during cranberry harvest at the field head-quarters. *Courtesy of the Whitesbog Preservation Trust.*

Frederick V. Coville and Elizabeth C. White inspecting blueberry bushes at Whitesbog. *Courtesy of Whitesbog Preservation Trust.*

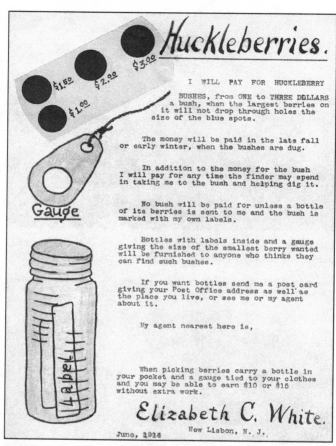

Poster soliciting locals to help in the search for large-fruited huckleberry (blueberry) bushes to be used in hybridization, 1914. *Courtesy of the Whitesbog Preservation Trust.*

Elizabeth C. White preparing blueberries to be photographed. A camera is located on the tripod under the dark cloth. *Courtesy of the Whitesbog Preservation Trust.*

Elizabeth C. White with families of seasonal cranberry pickers at evening entertainment, arranged by the padrone (picking boss) at Whitesbog. *Courtesy of the Whitesbog Preservation Trust.*

Elizabeth C. White examining a large Franklinia shrub at Whitesbog. *Courtesy of the Whitesbog Preservation Trust.*

Suningive at Whitesbog in 1928. *Courtesy of the Whitesbog Preservation Trust.*

The East garden at Suningive. *Courtesy of the Whitesbog Preservation Trust.*

Nancy Vail, June's sister, at Suningive. *Courtesy of Whitesbog Preservation Trust.*

June Vail, Elizabeth and children. *Courtesy of Whitesbog Preservation Trust.*

Photographic portrait of Elizabeth C. White. *Courtesy of the Whitesbog Preservation Trust.*

Appendix A
The White Family Line

The White family honored their ancestors by naming children for their forebearers. This resulted in a plethora of Josiahs, Barclays, Johns, Elizabeths, etc. It is hoped that the following listing will assist in clarifying family relationships. It is not meant to be a complete genealogy, but, rather, a record of family members encountered in the pages of this book.

1ST GENERATION
Christopher White (1642–1693) m. Hester Biddle. Arrived in West Jersey at Alloway Creek, Salem County, New Jersey, from England, June 28, 1677.

2ND GENERATION
Josiah White (1675–1713).

3RD GENERATION
Josiah White (June 21, 1705–May 12, 1780) m. Rebecca Foster. Farmer, dam engineer, fuller; moved from Salem to Mount Holly circa 1729.

4TH GENERATION
John White (July 9, 1747–August 21, 1785) m. Rebecca Powell.

5TH GENERATION

Josiah White (March 4, 1781–November 14, 1850). Founded the Lehigh Coal and Navigation Company.

Joseph White (December 28, 1785–May 25, 1827) m. Rebecca Smith. A successful entrepreneur, establishing a coal distribution network.

6TH GENERATION

John Josiah White (1808–1878) m. Mary Kirkbride Shoemaker. Son of Joseph and Rebecca S. White.

Barclay White (1821–1906) m. (1) Rebecca Merritt Lamb; m. (2) Beulah Shreve; (3) Adele Wills. Son of Joseph and Rebecca S. White. Owner of SHARON farm.

7TH GENERATION

Howard White (1844–1916) m. Helen T. Comly. Son of Barclay and Rebecca M. L. White.

Joseph Josiah (J. J.) White (1846–1924) m. Mary Anne Fenwick. Son of Barclay and Rebecca M. L. White.

George Foster White (1847–1928) m. Mary Jeanes Walter. Son of Barclay and Rebecca M. L. White.

Barclay White (1850–1877) m. unknown. Son of Barclay and Rebecca M. L. White.

Daniel White (1853–1935) m. Serena Bremer Green. Son of Barclay White and Beulah S. White. Owner of Traymore Hotel in Atlantic City.

Josiah White (1841–1914) m. Mary Kirby Allen. Son of John J. and Mary K. S. White. Owner of Marlborough-Blenheim Hotel in Atlantic City. Took part in 1904 Mediterranean trip.

8TH GENERATION

Elizabeth Coleman White (October 5, 1871–November 27, 1954). Daughter of J. J. and Mary A. F. White.

Mary F. (1873–1953) m. Emlen Darlington. Daughter of J. J. and Mary A. F. White.

Beulah S. (1875–1952) m. Lewis W. Darlington. Daughter of J. J. and Mary A. F. White.

Anne P. (1882–1956) m. Franklin S. Chambers. Daughter of J. J. and Mary A. F. White.

Frances Maria White (1869–1958). Daughter of cousin Josiah White and Mary K. A. White.

Gertrude Allen White (1880–1930). Daughter of cousin Josiah White and Mary K. A. White.

9TH GENERATION

Joseph W. Darlington (1917–1948) m. Mary Ellis. Son of Lewis W. Darlington and Beulah S. W. Darlington. President Joseph J. White, Inc., 1947–48.

Thomas B. Darlington (1924–2008) m. Martha Burton. Son of Lewis W. Darlington and Beulah S. W. Darlington. President Joseph J. White, Inc., 1952–1995.

Elizabeth H. Chambers (1909–??). Daughter of Frank and Anne White Chambers.

10TH GENERATION

Joseph W. Darlington m. Brenda Conner. Son of Thomas and Martha B. Darlington. Current President Joseph J. White, Inc.

A Partial Direct-line Pedigree of the White Ancestors

Christopher White (1642–1693) m. Hester Biddle

Josiah White (1675–1713) m. unknown

Josiah White (1705–1780) m. Rebecca Foster

John White (1747–1785) m. Rebecca Powell

Joseph White (1785–1827) m. Rebecca Smith

Barclay White (1821–1906) m. 1. Rebecca Merritt Lamb;
2. Beulah Shreve; (3) Adele Wills
Barclay White was Superintendent of Indian Affairs during the administration of Ulysses S. Grant.

Joseph Josiah White (1846–1924) m. Mary Anne
Fenwick

Elizabeth Coleman White, unmarried
Mary F. White m. Emlen Darlington
Beulah S. White m. Lewis W. Darlington
Anne P. White m. Franklin S. Chambers

Thomas B. Darlington m. Martha Burton

Joseph W. Darlington m. Brenda Conner

A Partial Direct-line Pedigree of the Fenwick Ancestors

Cuthbert Fenwick (1614–1645) m. Jane Eltonhead
Jane Eltonhead's sister Martha was the great great grandmother of President James Madison.

Richard Fenwick (c. 1653–1714) m. Priscilla Ann Bent

Ignatius Fenwick (1673–c. 1732) m. Eleanor Clarke

Ignatius Fenwick (1712–1776) m. Mary Cole

Capt. James Fenwick (1749–1806) m. Catherine Ford

Lt. Col. Athanasius Fenwick (1780–1824) m.
Susanna Howell
Susan Howell's sister, Mary, was the wife of Benjamin Jones, the builder and original owner of Fenwick Manor.)

James Athanasius Fenwick (1818–1882) m. Mary E. Cashell
These were the first Fenwicks to live in Fenwick Manor, present home of the Pinelands Commission.

Mary Anne Fenwick (1847–1922) m. Joseph Josiah
White

Elizabeth Coleman White

Appendix B
Awards and Recognitions

1912 First woman member of The American Cranberry Growers' Association.

1913 Named President of the Board of Lady Visitors of Four Mile Colony; served in this capacity until 1916, when the state took over the Colony and the Board of Lady Visitors was dissolved.

1916 Appointed to the Board of Directors of the New Jersey State Colony for Boys (originally called Four Mile Colony and currently, New Lisbon Developmental Center). Active member of the Board 1916–1949; member emeritus 1950–1954; at various times served as vice-president and secretary.

1920 Awarded the Bronze Wilder Medal of the American Pomological Society at its meeting in Ohio for "Exhibit of Blueberries."

1927 Organized and named a Director of the Blueberry Co-operative Association of New Jersey.

1929 First woman President of The American Cranberry Growers' Association.

1932 First recipient of a citation from the New Jersey State Board of Agriculture for "Outstanding Contributions to Agriculture in New Jersey."**

1934 First woman member of the Philadelphia Society for Promoting Agriculture.

1941 Awarded the Gold Medal of the Massachusetts Horticultural Society for "Valuable Service in behalf of Horticulture."

1946 Granted honorary lifetime membership in the Blueberry Co-operative Association of New Jersey.

1947 Became a charter member of the Holly Society of America.

1952 Awarded the Silver Wilder Medal of the American Pomological Society at its meeting in Roanoke, Virginia, with the citation "Plant breeder, horticulturist, scientist through whose skill and zeal the blueberry has been markedly improved as a horticultural crop."

1953 Awarded an inscribed silver bowl by the Blueberry Institute.

1954 Awarded a stained-glass Holly Plaque at the spring meeting of the Holly Society of America.

1966 'Elizabeth' blueberry selected and named by the New Jersey Cultivated Blueberry Council.

n.d. Honorary member of the Garden Clubs of New Jersey.

** Elizabeth White shared the honor of being the first to receive this award with Edward A. Sexsmith, who was recognized for his reorganization of the New Jersey Department of Agriculture.

Appendix C
Holly Varieties

Holly Variety	Gender	Selected / Introduced by Elizabeth C. White
Argentine	F	Selected at Holly Haven c. 1953
Betsy	F	Selected 1935–1940 with T. Windon Introduced by ECW in 1948
Clark	F	'White Hedge'; selected circa 1930
Delia	F	Selected 1935–1940 with T. Windon
Earl	F	Selected Lippincott Property in Pemberton circa 1930
Farage	F	Found wild in New Lisbon, moved to Whitesbog before 1942
Goldie	F	Discovered by Mrs. W. K. DuPont in DE; introduced by ECW 1940
Griscom	F	Sel. Woodbury, NJ, by ECW & Griscom; intro by ECW circa 1930
Halcyon	F	Selected 1935–1940 with T. Windon
Halstead		Circa 1930 in NJ
Harry	M	No information available
Hopkins	F	Origin in NJ before 1949
Isaiah	M	Selected before 1948; tree on Whitesbog farm
John Higgins	M	Selected before 1949
Joyce	F	Selected 1935–1940 with T. Windon
Karen	F	Selected 1935–1940; near Whitesbog with T. Windon

Laura	F	Selected 1935–1940 with T. Windon
Mae	F	Selected 1935–1940 with T. Windon
Manig	F	Selected 1935–1940 with T. Windon
Osa	F	Selected 1935–1940 with T. Windon
Reeve East	F	Selected in 1953
Reeve West	F	Selected in 1953
Sallie	F	'Aalto No. 2'; 'Sally'; 'Wheeler No. 2'; selected in NJ before 1948
Sara Higgins	F	Selected E. C. White; introduced Holly Haven 1951
Shreve	F	HSA Bulletin No. 6; selected circa 1930
Slim Jim	M	Selected circa 1940 with T. Windon
Stanley	M	HSA Bulletin No. 6; selected circa 1930
Susan	F	Origin near New Lisbon; selected 1920–1923
Vivian	F	Selected 1935–1940 with T. Windon

Holly Variety	Gender	Selected by Elizabeth C. White and Wilfrid Wheeler
Beulah	F	'Boyden No. 3'; selected before 1953
Fay	F	'Aalto No. 14'; selected before 1953
Harriet	F	'Aalto No. 2'; selected 1942 in MA
John Banks	M	'Wheeler No. 9'; selected before 1947
Kate	F	'Aalto No. 3'; selected before 1953 near Whitesbog, NJ
Laura Thomas	F	Selected 1941 in Osterville, MA
Makepeace	M	'Ed Thomas'; selected before 1953
Muriel	F	Noted in HSA Bulletin No. 6, 1953
Nash	M	HSA Proceedings 1953; selected 1940
Nell	F	'Aalto No. 15'; HSA Bulletin No. 6
Nora	F	Selected by Wheeler, White and W. Boyden in MA
Pauline	F	No date available
Perpetual	F	'Boyden No. 6'; selected before 1953 origin Sandwich, MA
Quinn	M	HSA Proceedings 1948
Sibyl	F	'Aalto No. 10'; HSA Bulletin No. 6
Tiny	F	'Ashumet No. 23'; 'Petite'; selected before 1953
Vera	F	'Boyden No. 2'; selected before 1953 from wild on Cape Cod, MA
Zoe	F	'Boyden No. 1'; selected before 1953 in MA

Bibliography of Books Consulted

Bailey, L. H., ed. *Standard Cyclopedia of Horticulture*. NY: The Macmillan Company, 1917.

Boyd, Howard P. *A Field Guide to the Pine Barrens of New Jersey*. Medford, NJ: Plexus Publishing, 1991.

Carroll, Charles A. *Hard Candy*. Freedonia, WI: Champion Press, Ltd., 2005.

Coville, Frederick V. *Experiments in Blueberry Culture, U.S. Department of Agriculture, Bureau of Plant Industry, Bulletin 193*. Washington, D.C., November 1910.

_____. *Directions For Blueberry Culture. U.S. Department of Agriculture, Bureau of Plant Industry, Bulletin 334*. Washington, D.C., December 29, 1915.

_____. *Early Experiments With Blueberries Culture. U.S. Department of Agriculture, Bureau of Plant Industry, Bulletin 974*. Washington, D.C., October 1921.

Devery, B. C. *The Story of Four Mile Colony*. Published for the Twenty-Fifth Anniversary of the New Jersey State Colony, New Lisbon, New Jersey, 1939.

Dye, Franklin, Secretary. *Eighteenth Annual Report of the State Board of Agriculture*. Trenton, NJ: The John L. Murphy Publishing Company, 1891.

Eck, Paul. *The American Cranberry*. New Brunswick, NJ: Rutgers University Press, 1990.

Eck, Paul, and Norman F. Childers, eds. *Blueberry Culture*. New Brunswick, NJ: Rutgers University Press, 1966.

Forman, Richard T. T. *Pine Barrens: Ecosystem and Landscape*. New York: Academic Press Inc., 1979.

Freedman, Russell. *Kids at Work: Lewis Hine and the Crusade Against Child Labor.* NY: Clarion Books, 1994.

Galle, Fred C. *Hollies, The Genus Ilex.* Portland, OR: Timber Press, 1997.

Hahamovitch, Cindy. *The Fruits of Their Labors.* Chapel Hill, NC: The University of North Carolina Press, 1997.

Hindman, Hugh D. *Child Labor: An American History.* Armonk, NY: M.E. Sharpe, 2002.

Historic American Landscapes Survey, Whitesbog Village and Cranberry Bog, HALS No. NJ-1. View at the Historic American Landscapes Survey, Library of Congress.

Hume, H. Harold. *Hollies.* NY: The Macmillan Company, 1953.

McPhee, John. *The Pine Barrens.* NY: Farrar, Straus and Giroux, 1968.

Morton, Eleanor. *Josiah White: Prince of Pioneers.* NY: Stephen Daye Press, 1946.

Olsen, Judith Lamb. *Pemberton: an Historic Look At a Village On the Rancocas.* New Orleans, LA: Polyanthos, Inc., 1976.

Reeves, Robert M. *A Reeves' Account of New Lisbon.* Ed., Chelsea Karlberg. Lulu, Inc., 2009.

Trattner, Walter I. *A History of the National Child Labor Committee and Child Labor Reform in America.* Chicago, IL: Quadrangle Books, 1970.

White, Elizabeth C. "Cranberries." *Standard Cyclopedia of Horticulture.* Vol. 2. NY: Macmillan, 1917, 732–34.

White, Joseph J. *Cranberry Culture.* NY: O. Judd Company, 1870.

Wildman, Edward Embree. *Penn's Woods 1682–1932.* Philadelphia: Christopher Sower Company, 1933.

Magazine Articles and Manuscripts Consulted

Chambers, Franklin S. "Remarks on Whitesbog History." *Proceedings of the 50th Annual Convention, American Cranberry Growers Association* (August 1919), 9–10.

Chute, Charles. "Cost of the Cranberry Sauce." *The Survey* (December 2, 1911).

Ciotola, Nicholas. "From Philadelphia to the Pinelands: The New Jersey Photographs of Lewis W. Hine." *The Pennsylvania Magazine of History and Biography* 137, no. 2 (April 2013), 179–90.

Clark, J. Harold. "Miss Elizabeth White Is a Horticultural Pioneer." *Horticultural News* 27, no. 2 (February 1946), 1799–1801.

Collingswood, H. H. "The Blueberry Lady." *Country Life in America* (September 1916).

Coville, Frederick V. "The Wild Blueberry Tamed." *The National Geographic Magazine* (June 1916).

Coville, Frederick V. "Improving the Wild Blueberry." *U.S. Department of Agriculture, Bureau of Plant Industry Yearbook 1937*, 559–74.

Dammann, Louis. *My Autobiography Book #2*. Courtesy of Egg Harbor City Historical Society, Egg Harbor City, NJ.

Darke, Rick. "Beauty in the Barrens." *The American Gardner* 79, no. 3 (May/June 2000), 36–42.

Elmendorf, Augustine. "The Cranberry Bogs of Burlington County, New Jersey," typescript, 1914. Whitesbog Preservation Trust Archives.

Fair, Laura, B. S. "Migrants As a Social and Educational Problem In New Jersey." *Rutgers University Bulletin*, Series 8, no. 11a (May 1932).

Ginger, Mina C. "In Berry Field and Bog." *The Railroad Trainman's Journal* 23, no. 6 (June 1906), 475–81.

Hambridge, Gove. "The Story of Elizabeth C. White: She Makes a Handsome Living Growing Blueberries." *Success* [New York] (October 1927).

Hobson, Asher. "Study of Cooperative Marketing." *Better Fruit* (December 1922).

Jenkins, Charles F. "The Historical Background of Franklin's Tree." *The Pennsylvania Magazine of History and Biography* 57, no. 3 (November 1933): 193–208.

Kite, Elizabeth S. "The 'Pineys.'" *The Survey* (October 4, 1913).

Lovejoy, Owen. "The Cost of the Cranberry Sauce." *The Survey* (January 6, 1911).

MacCulloch, Campbell. "Who Picked Your Cranberry Sauce?" *Good Housekeeping* (November 1913).

McFarland, J. Horace. "Blueberries." Whitesbog Blueberries, Joseph J. White, Inc., New Lisbon, NJ, 1921.

New Jersey State Archives. Monthly Reports of Children's Guardians 1899–1956. Series SINCG004, Trenton, NJ.

New Jersey State Archives. Monthly Reports of the Department of Institutions and Agencies 1926–1971. Series SIN00001, Trenton, NJ.

Nixon, Virginia. "Blueberries as Big as Grapes." *The Forecast* [New York] August 1923.

Platt, Polly. "White Soars to Fame on Blueberries and Hollies." *The Sunday Bulletin* [Philadelphia] December 11, 1949.

Presbyterian Historical Society Archives. Field Notes of Home Mission Council of North America 1903–1951. Box 13, Folders 5-11, Philadelphia, PA.

Proceedings of the Forty-Third Annual Convention of the American Cranberry Growers' Association, August 24, 1912.

Proceedings of the Forty-Sixth Annual Convention of the American Cranberry Growers Association, August 27, 1915.

Proceedings of the Sixtieth Annual Meeting of the American

Cranberry Growers Association, January 25, 1930.

Proceedings of the Sixty-First Annual Meeting of the American Cranberry Growers Association, January 31, 1931.

Proceedings of the First Annual Conference of the Women's National Agricultural and Horticultural Association, May 1, 1914.

Raymond, Dorothea F. "Migrants in Cranberries in New Jersey," Council of Women For Home Missions, New York, NY, undated.

Reasoner, Arlene. "New Jersey Blueberry Industry." *Journal of Industry and Finance* 13, no. 4 (March 1939).

Report of the Investigations Conducted by Public Education and Child labor Associations of Pennsylvania, 1915, Whitesbog Preservation Trust Archives.

Rose, Philip S. "The Blueberry Queen." *The Saturday Evening Post* (September 12, 1942).

Saretzky, Gary. "Nineteenth Century New Jersey Photographers." *New Jersey History* [Newark, New Jersey] (Fall/ Winter 2004), 36–143.

Scoglio, Jeanette E. "The White Family History." A History Seminar Paper Presented to Albright College, April 12, 1966.

Stevens, Neil H. "Some Cranberry Growers I Have Known." *Cranberries, The National Magazine* (February 1937).

White, Joseph J. "Cranberry Culture." New Lisbon, NJ, 1914, Whitesbog Preservation Trust Archives.

Woodward, Carl R. "Blueberries an Inch Across." *The Country Gentleman* (November 11, 1922).

Correspondence Consulted

Correspondence Joseph J. White and Owen Lovejoy, Whitesbog Preservation Trust Archives.

Correspondence James A. Fenwick to Benjamin and Andrew Jones 1840–1882, Whitesbog Preservation Trust Archives.

Elizabeth C. White Manuscripts / Addresses

"Blueberry Culture." *Bulletin of the American Rock Garden Society* 1, no. 3 (May–June 1943), 53-56.

"Cranberries and Colony Contributions or the Appeal of the Colony to a Dweller in the Pines." Transcript of address read before the New Jersey Conference of Charities and Corrections at Asbury Park, NJ, April 24, 1914, 24 pp. Whitesbog Preservation Trust Archives.

"Cultured Blueberries." *Plants and Gardens* [Brooklyn Botanic Gardens] 3, New Series, no. 1 (Spring 1947), 41–45.

"Development of the Cultivated Blueberry." Transcript of address read before the American Pomological Society December, 1920. Whitesbog Preservation Trust Archives.

"Development of the Cultivated Blueberry." *Hoosier Horticulture. Monthly Publication of Indiana Horticultural Society*, 3, no. 12 (December 1921).

"Discoveries." *Proceedings of the Fifty-Ninth Annual Convention of the American Cranberry Growers Association* (August 30, 1929).

"An Experimental Farm in Miniature." J. J, White, Inc., New Lisbon, 1926. Whitesbog Preservation Trust Archives.

"A History of Whitesbog." *Proceedings of the Seventy-Second Annual Convention of the American Cranberry Growers Association* (August 28, 1941).

"Housing and Care of Cranberry Pickers." *Proceedings of the Forty-Third Annual Convention of the American Cranberry Growers Association* (August 24, 1912).

"My Garden of Pine Barren Plants." Transcript of Program of the Garden Club of New Jersey broadcast over WOR, Newark NJ, March 24, 1941, 5 pp. Whitesbog Preservation Trust Archives.

Personal Correspondence with Jane Addams, Hull House, Chicago, Illinois, January 9,1911.

Personal Correspondence with Wilfrid Wheeler, Ashumet Farm, Falmouth, MA, 1938–1954.

"The Pineys of New Jersey." Paper read at meeting of the Nassau Chapter of Daughters of American Revolution (DAR), Camden, January 13, 1917. Whitesbog Preservation Trust Archives.

"Plants of the New Jersey Pine Barrens." *Quarterly Bulletin of Woman's National Farm and Garden Association* 3, no. 3 (February 1917): 3–10.

"Presidential Address." *Proceedings of the Sixtieth Annual Meeting of the American Cranberry Growers Association* (January 25, 1930).

"Some Results of Self-Pollination of the Highbush Blueberry at Whitesbog, New Jersey." *Proceedings of the American Society for Horticultural Science* 36, 1938.

"The Story of Gordonia." *Pennsylvania Gardens* 1, no. 2 (June 1917), 14–17.

"A Talk About Cultivated Blueberry." *The Rural New Yorker* (April 3, 1920).

"Taming Blueberries." Transcript of Program of the Garden Club of New Jersey broadcast over WOR, Newark NJ, July 6, 1937.

"Taming the Blueberry." *American Fruit Grower* (June 1920).

"The 25th Anniversary of the Beginning of Blueberry Culture at Whitesbog." *Cranberries: The National Cranberry Magazine* (January–May, 1936).

Endnotes

With sadness we inform readers that Albertine Senske, author of this biography and, for nearly two decades, archivist of the Whitesbog Preservation Trust, died in 2018. At that time the text was complete, but not all citations were finalized. Whitesbog staff and editors have worked to fill the gaps, but without Albertine's extraordinarily comprehensive knowledge of Elizabeth Coleman White, a small number of references remain incomplete, as indicated in the endnotes. In these places we ask that readers trust Albertine's research judgment.

Foreword

1. Told at a gathering celebrating the fiftieth anniversary of the American Cranberry Growers' Association. Frank Chambers was J. J. White's son-in-law and Elizabeth's brother-in-law; Chambers was future successor to J. J. White as President of Joseph J. White, Inc.

2. *Proceedings of Wisconsin*, 27.

3. For simplicity's sake, we will use the name Whitesbog throughout these pages to refer to the cranberry farm James Fenwick established and J. J. White later expanded and developed. The name actually came into existence in 1923 when a third-class post office opened in the village.

4. There are several theories about the origin of the name, but nothing definitive. An estate encountered in her European travels; a return address on a letter received; a name seen in a poem are a few of the supposed sources of the name "Suningive."

5. Neil Stevens, "Some Cranberry Growers I Have Known," *Cranberries, The National Cranberry Magazine* (February 1937): 8. The Scriptural quotation is from Ecclesiastes 9:10.

Elizabeth C. White: Whose Child is This?

6. Appendix A contains an abbreviated family tree that shows the direct line from Christopher White to Joseph Darlington, current president of Joseph J. White, Inc.

7. The West Jersey Council of Proprietors divided its territory into tenths. John Fenwick acquired title to the Fifth or Salem Tenth, which occupied much of the present-day counties of Salem and Cumberland. This Fenwick is not directly related to Elizabeth's maternal grandfather Fenwick.

8. Date found on Internet, based on data contained in William Wade Hinshaw and Thomas Worth Marshall, *Encyclopedia of American Quaker Genealogy*, vol. II (Baltimore: Genealogical Pub., Co., 1969).

9. Thomas Shourds, *History and Genealogy of Fenwick's Colony* (Bridgeton, NJ: George F. Nixon, 1876), 308–24.

10. Henry C. Shinn, *The History of Mount Holly* (Mount Holly, NJ: The Mount Holly Herald, [1957]), 11.

11. Ibid.

12. See "Cranberry Culture by Joseph J. White," hand-dated October 15, 1914, WPT archives: 1984.4.4. Sim Place today is part of the Haines and Haines cranberry farm.

13. This account is extracted from Elizabeth White's commentary on and expansion of Fenwick family history as garnered from James Fenwick's letters to his uncle, Benjamin Jones, and cousin, Andrew Jones.

14. Pierson Coleman was the son of Ann Coleman, the woman who raised Mary Cashell Fenwick.

The Early Years

15. Elizabeth C. White, personal letters, WPT.

16. Elizabeth C. White, "Some Bog Plants of the Jersey Pines," *Wise-Acres*, publication of the Pennsylvania School of Horticulture for Women (Ambler, PA, 1929): 70–71.

17. Elizabeth C. White, personal letters, WPT.

18. "A History of Whitesbog," *Proceedings of the Seventy-Second Annual Convention of the American Cranberry Growers Association* (August 28, 1941).

19. "A History of Whitesbog," *Proceedings of the Seventy-Second Annual Convention of the American Cranberry Growers Association* (August 28, 1941).

A Love of Learning

20. From "Cranberries and Colony Contributions," 3; copy at WPT archives. On April 21, 1914, Elizabeth addressed the annual meeting of the New Jersey Commission of Charities and Corrections, presenting a paper entitled "Cranberries and Colony Contributions." It was reprinted in pamphlet form.

21. Orthography is the art of writing words with the proper letters according to standard usage. Its study includes rules of spelling, hyphenation, capitalization, word breaks, and punctuation.

22. Personal diary of Beulah S. White, 1916.

23. Document ID 1984.2.5, WPT archives.

24. Letter from J. J. on Growers official letterhead dated Dec. 16, 1910, WPT archives.

25. Local Quaker businessmen funded and opened both Hahnemann and Women's Medical Hospitals. This may have made one of these two establishments a likely choice for Elizabeth White's training.

Elizabeth White the Horticulturist: Cranberries 101

26. Personal diary of Beulah S. White, entry for March 6, 1912.

27. 'Howe' is a variety of cranberry selected from the wild and propagated by Elias Howe of Massachusetts.

28. Elizabeth C. White, "Discoveries," *Proceedings of the 59th Annual Convention of the American Cranberry Growers Association* (August 30, 1929).

29. Details from an undated and unsigned biographical sketch that paints Elizabeth White's life in broad strokes, covering the usual material. There are several inaccuracies that are based on oral lore rather than empirical research. Examples include White's education, ownership of Fenwick Manor, religion of parents and involvement of Four Mile Colony. The author uses direct quotations to substantiate several statements. WPT archives: 1984.2.6.

30. This account is extracted from Elizabeth's personal notes, found between the letters of James Fenwick to his cousin Jones.

31. Gove Hambridge, "She Makes a Handsome Living Growing Blueberries," *Success Magazine* (October 1927), 40.

32. Elizabeth C. White, "Cranberries and Colony Contributions." Read before the New Jersey Conference of Charities and Correction, Asbury Park, NJ, April 21, 1914, 3–4.

33. Elizabeth C. White, "Reminiscences of Whitesbog," *Proceedings of the 72nd Annual Convention of the American Cranberry Growers Association*, August 28, 1941.

34. Manuscript in Whitesbog Preservation Trust Archives, 1984.2.27. See also Elizabeth C. White, "Reminiscences of Whitesbog," *Proceedings of the 72nd Annual Convention of the American Cranberry Growers Association*, August 28, 1941.

35. Elizabeth C. White, "Book Review of *Prince of Pioneers*," 3. Eleanor Morton, *Josiah White: Prince of Pioneers* (New York: Stephen Daye Press, 1946).

36. Elizabeth C. White, "Reminiscences of Whitesbog," *Proceedings of the 72nd Annual Convention of the American Cranberry Growers Association*, August 28, 1941.

37. American Cranberry Growers Association (ACGA) was the New Jersey self-help group formed in 1869 by T. Budd, J. Fenwick, B. White, et al.

38. It is interesting to note that Frank Chambers, who first entered the cranberry community in 1911, became a member at the same time.

39. Elizabeth C. White, "Discoveries," *Proceedings of the 59th Annual Convention of the American Cranberry Growers Association*, August 30, 1929.

40. Ibid.

41. *Proceedings of the Fiftieth Annual Convention of the American Cranberry Growers Association*, August 23, 1919, 6.

An Adventure in Blue

42. Although in the Middle Atlantic States wild blueberries were called "swamp huckleberries" or simply "huckleberries," the huckleberry is a distinct fruit of the genus *Gaylussacia*, related to the blueberry of the genus *Vaccinium*. What the Pineys called wild huckleberry was actually the native Northern highbush blueberry, *Vaccinium coybosum*.

43. Elizabeth C. White, *Plants and Gardens* 3, no. 1 (Spring 1947): 42.

44. Regretfully, no citation has been identified for Covill's handwritten note.

45. Frederick V. Coville, "Experiments in Blueberry Culture," *Bulletin 193*, 80–81.

46. Ibid, 89.

47. Elizabeth C. White mentions that the locals vied to be the first and best providers of berries to the resorts. Her father knew this and gave his workers off at the beginning of the picking season since he knew they would not arrive in any case. The Buzby's Chatsworth General Store collection preserved in Stockton University's Bjork Library, Special Collections, has records of huckleberries sold by the quart to

fruit sellers in New York City and Mount Holly dated 1902.

48. Elizabeth C. White, "The Development of Blueberry Culture," Address before the Philadelphia Society for Promoting Agriculture, April 17, 1934.

49. *Proceedings of the Fiftieth Annual Convention of the American Cranberry Growers Association*, 1919, 12.

50. Letter from Elizabeth C. White to B. T. Galloway, Chief, Bureau of Plant Industry, U.S. Department of Agriculture. January 11, 1911. WPT archives.

51. Elizabeth C. White. "The 25th Anniversary of the Beginning of Blueberry Culture at Whitesbog, New Jersey." *Cranberries The National Magazine*, May 1936, 14.

52. Regretfully, no citation has been identified for Coville's return letter to Elizabeth setting up their first meeting.

53. Elizabeth C. White. "The 25th Anniversary of the Beginning of Blueberry Culture at Whitesbog, New Jersey." *Cranberries The National Magazine*, May 1936, 14.

54. Wisconsin, 27.

55. Sooy found two additional bushes in 1911, hence the numbering indicating order discovered.

56. This citation almost certainly can be found in Elizabeth White's small spindle notebooks in the WPT archives.

57. Cf. *Cranberries, The National Magazine* (June 1936): 11.

58. Elizabeth White was an equal opportunity employer. Theodore Dunfee was only ten years old.

59. *Trenton Evening News*, July 12, 1951, 30.

60. This citation almost certainly can be found in Elizabeth White's small spindle notebooks in the WPT archives.

61. When identifying the parents of hybrid plants, the first cultivar named represents the male contributor and the second cultivar is the female. Note that for 'Pioneer' and 'Katharine,' the same cultivars were used but in opposite roles.

62. Charles Beckwith, New Jersey Agricultural Experiment Stations Circular 170.

63. Until 1925, all sales were "mixed" fruit: 'Rubels,' named hybrids, and test berries.

64. *Proceedings of the Fifty-Third Annual Meeting of the American Cranberry Growers Association*, 1924, 11. Within the same report White notes that Whitesbog Blueberry plants had already been shipped across the United States and Canada as well as a few shipments to Europe.

65. Joseph J. White Ledger shows advertising costs from 1921 to 1927 were slightly under $26,000.

66. Blueberry Growers mentioned were Mr. Scammell and Mr. Waite of Toms River, Mr. Bishop of Indian Mills, Dr. Darlington (probably Emlen), and Mr. Stanley Coville of New Lisbon.

67. Regretfully, no citation has been identified for the *Try and Report Plan*.

68. The account of Louis Dammann is recorded in volume 2 of his handwritten autobiography which the Egg Harbor City Historical Society shared with the author.

69. "Preparation of Selling Plans for Whitesbog Blueberry Plants. . . ." WPT archives: 69:1984.1.82.

70. Elizabeth C. White, "Beginning of Blueberry Culture," *Cranberries Magazine* 4 (1936): 18.

71. In 1938 White noted that excessive rains, amounting to 4.85 inches between July 16 and 22, affected both the amount of sugar as well as aroma in berries picked after that date, which, in turn, would have had a market effect. (General growing notes cataloged in Whitesbog Archives.)

72. Data in the table below was taken from the ledgers of Joseph J. White, Inc.

73. "The 25th Anniversary of the Beginning of Blueberry Culture at Whitesbog, New Jersey," *The Blueberry Grower* [May 1936], 14. WPT archives: 74:1984.1.1.

74. Ibid., 15.

75. "Development of Wild Blueberry Into an Aristocrat

of Fruits Is Achievement of Burlington Woman," *Newark Evening News*, November 1, 1924.

76. *Cranberries, the National Magazine*, May 1936, 14–15.

77. Elizabeth C. White, "The Pineys." Speech given by Elizabeth C. White to the Camden Chapter of the Daughters of the American Revolution in 1917.

Holly Haven

78. Information obtained from Windon's son. Attempted verification of University of Massachusetts attendance did not find Windon enrolled in the School of Agriculture between 1915 and 1920. However, a Thomas Window is listed as a member of the graduating class of 1917 which would be the right time frame for Windon (1897–1965).

79. Beulah and Lewis Darlington had three sons: Joe, Lewis who died in infancy, and Tom.

80. Very little has been verified about Jacob Homer other than he was a teacher from Grasmere, New York.

81. Meeting notes between Jacob Homer and Thomas B. Darlington, August 10, 1950. WPT archives: 1984.3.55.

82. Brochure: "The Elizabeth C. White Story," WPT archives: 1984.3.77.

83. Brochure: "The Elizabeth C. White Story," WPT archives: 1984.3.51.

84. A copy of Elizabeth C. White's will can be found in the Whitesbog archives: WPT archives: 1984.2.20.

85. To select means to identify a holly as suitable for commercial cultivation; to introduce means to be the first to offer a selection for public purchase.

June Vail

86. Interview with Martha Windisch, *Whitesbog Preservation Trust Newsletter*, 1st Quarter, 2013, 5.

Franklinia

87. John Bartram, *Diary of a Journey through the Carolinas, Georgia and Florida: July 1, 1765 to April 10, 1766* (Philadelphia: The American Philosophical Society, 1942).

88. William Bartram, *Travels with William Bartram*, ed. Mark Van Doren (New York: Dover Publications, 1929).

89. Moses Marshall was the nephew and business associate of Humphry Marshall, a younger cousin of John Bartram and another of the group of Quaker botanists located in Chester County, Pennsylvania. In 1764, Humphry Marshall constructed a conservatory on his farm for the culture of rare plants.

90. Elizabeth C. White, "The Story of Gordonia," *Pennsylvania Gardens* 1, no. 2 (June 1937), The Pennsylvania Horticultural Society, 14–17.

Elizabeth's Nurseries

91. Regretfully, no citation has been identified for Elizabeth's sales guarantee.

Elizabeth C. White the Social Advocate

92. Cindy Hahamovitch, *The Fruits of Their Labor: Atlantic Coast Farmworkers and the Making of Migrant Poverty, 1870–1945* (Chapel Hill and London: University of North Carolina Press, 1997), 30.

93. Early Blacks, also known as Dark Reds, was a variety of cranberry that ripened early and usually harvested first in New Jersey.

94. Elizabeth White, *Cranberries and Colony Contributions*, 5. The photographer was Lewis Hine.

95. The National Child Labor Committee (NCLC) is a private, non-profit organization in the United States founded in New York in 1904 to promote the rights, well-being, and education of children and youth as they relate to work and working.

96. Writing to Cleland of immigration, Elizabeth White thanks him for Ginger's article and says she read it with interest. This would seem to imply she had never seen it before. However, someone in the cranberry community appears to have been aware of Ginger's study, for she quotes a cranberry owner who estimated that $250,000 went back to Philadelphia each year by cranberry pickers alone.

97. Elizabeth C. White, "Cranberries and Colony Contributions: Or The Appeal of the Colony to a Dweller in the Pines." Read before the New Jersey Conference of Charities and Correction at Asbury Park, N.J., April 21, 1914, 5–6. WPT.

98. Edward T. Devine (1867–1948) was a native of Iowa who became an influential economist, child welfare advocate, educator, author, and pioneer social worker. He was also a member of the Board of Trustees of the NCLC. It is unknown why J. J. White selected him.

99. Whitesbog Preservation Trust Archives, Series of Letters between J. J. White and Owen Lovejoy, Secretary General of NCLC, WPT archives: 1984.12.23.

100. The series of letters between White and Lovejoy can be found in the Whitesbog Archives Heritage Collection of Documents.

101. Elizabeth C. White, "Cranberries and Colony Contributions: Or The Appeal of the Colony to a Dweller in the Pines," Read before the New Jersey Conference of Charities and Correction at Asbury Park, N.J., April 21, 1914, 6. WPT. Madonna House was a Roman Catholic service organization dedicated to providing religious support and guidance to the immigrant community as well as providing instruction and assistance in integrating into life in an urban and industrial society.

102. "Communications," *The Survey* (Jan. 28, 1911), 711.

103. Letter from Elizabeth C. White to Jane Addams, January 9, 1911. WPT archives: 1984.12.24.

104. Elizabeth C. White letter to Jane Addams, January 9, 1911, 1. Whitesbog Preservation Trust Archives.

105. *Proceedings of the Forty-Third Annual Convention of the American Cranberry Growers' Association* (August 24, 1912): 5–6, 14–15.

106. Rev. Augustine Elmendorf, "The Cranberry Bogs."

107. *Trenton Times Historic Archive*; published as *Trenton Evening Times*, March 22, 1911, 11. White may have used the photos during her talk. There is no mention of a formal exhibit in the Conference Program as there is of the NCLC display.

108. Charles L. Chute, "Cost of the Cranberry Sauce," *The Survey* (December 2, 1911): 1281–84.

109. Campbell MacCulloch, *Good Housekeeping* (November 1913): 675.

110. According to White, the NCLC says the child shall not work while the Training School says the child shall work in a way and at things that best contribute to its welfare and happiness (4–5). The reader will have to make a personal assessment as to the validity of this comparison because of the difference in the social conditions of the children in the two groups.

111. *Trenton Times Historical Archive*; published as *Trenton Evening Times*, December 21, 1914, 3.

112. Whitesbog Preservation Archives, Document 184.2.21.

113. *Proceedings of the Forty-Sixth Annual Convention of the American Cranberry Growers Association*, 10–15. Rev. E. H. Durrell, the Association president, had his own solution to the child labor problem. "No more hand picking for me; no more families on my bogs; no more children; no more tramping over my vines," 15.

114. There was another motive in requesting the survey, more practical than altruistic. Bills were being presented to the New Jersey Agricultural Progress Association to prevent

the use of migratory labor.

115. *Proceedings of the Sixtieth Annual Meeting of the American Cranberry Growers Association* (January 25, 1930): 4.

116. *Proceedings of the Sixty-First Annual Meeting of the American Cranberry Growers Association* (January 31, 1931) 14–17. Harry Weiss was the regular statistician for the ACGA.

Addressing Needs: Education

117. Letter to Elizabeth C. White located in Whitesbog Preservation Trust Archives.

118. *Membership, Directory and Statistics of the Home Missions Council and Council of Women for Home Missions* (New York: Home Missions Council, 1921), 24. See also E. O. Watson, *Year Book of the Churches, 1921–22* (Washington, D.C.: The Federal Council of the Churches of Christ in America, 1922), 305.

119. Regretfully, no citation has been identified for this statement from The Council of Women for Home Missions.

120. The account is based on contents found in Box 33, Field Notes, Presbyterian Archives.

121. Note relating to Laura Fair Report. Whitesbog Preservation Archives, Document 1984.12.42.

122. Laura Fair, *Migrants as a Social and Educational Problem in New Jersey* (New Brunswick, NJ: School of Education, Rutgers University, 1932).

Addressing Needs: Housing

123. Herbert Hoover, *Public Papers of the Presidents of the United States: Herbert Hoover, Containing the Public Messages, Speeches, and Statements of the President January 1 to December 31, 1931* (Washington: DC: United States Government Printing Office, 1976), 422.

124. The reader may recall Mrs. Gilbreth as the mother in *Cheaper By The Dozen* who continued her husband's work

after his untimely death and who became an influential business woman in her own right.

125. Proceedings of President Hoover's Conference on Home Building and Home Ownership (Washington, D.C.: 1931), 208–209.

126. Presbyterian Archives, Box 13, Folder 7.

127. Presbyterian Archives, Box 13, Folder 7.

128. Until the mid-1920s, cranberries were routinely shipped in barrels that were constructed in this building during the off-season and stored in an adjacent structure until needed in the autumn.

129. *A "Good Neighbor Policy" in Action on a Wide Front among Migrants of New Jersey*, 5.

130. Ibid., 5.

131. Regretfully, no citation has been identified for the demands of the Home Mission Council.

132. Presbyterian Archives, Box 13, Folder 7.

Four Mile Colony

133. "Cranberries and Colony Contributions," 16.

134. B. C. Devery, *The Story of Four Mile Colony* (New Lisbon, NJ: Published for the Twenty-Fifth Anniversary of the New Jersey State Colony, 1939) 27.

135. Devery, *The Story of Four Mile Colony*, 70.

136. Robert M. Reeves, *A Reeves' Account of New Lisbon*, ed. Chelsea Karberg (Lulu, Inc., 2009), 59.

137. Fenwick Manor Minutes Book, Annual meeting 1929, 1936, 1937.

138. Parole was the term used to describe time away from the colony and was used for periodic visits with family or testing a resident's ability to move back into society; it was also used to describe release for youthful offenders.

139. New Jersey Archives, Department of Charities and Corrections—Commissioner Ellis notes for January 25, 1932.

140. Devery, *The Story of Four Mile Colony*, 76. Dr. & Mrs. Darlington refer to Elizabeth's sister, Mary, and her husband, Emlen.

141. Devery, *The Story of Four Mile Colony*, 57.

142. *Helonias bullata*, also known as swamp pink, a rare herb native to the eastern United States.

143. Letter from Elizabeth Kite to Elizabeth C. White, May 3, [1931]. WPT archives: 1984.2.33.

144. Charles A. Carroll, *Hard Candy: Nobody Ever Flies Over the Cuckoo's Nest: A True Story* (Fredonia, WI: Champion Press Ltd., 2005). 8.

Elizabeth White the Naturalist, The Beauty of the Pines
145. Letter from Elizabeth S. Kite to Elizabeth C. White, May 3, 1931. WPT archives.

This chapter was previously published in *SoJourn*, and is well-illustrated with color photographs of many of the plants and flowers here described, from the collection of Pine Barrens historian Ted Gordon: see "Elizabeth C. White's Garden," *SoJourn* 2.2 (Winter 2017–18), 28–38.

146. "Mrs. B. B. Locke Named Chairman of Garden Days," *Trenton Sunday Times*, January 30, 1938, part two, 3.

147. Elizabeth C. White, "My Garden of Pine Barren Plants," mss. for program of the Radio Garden Club of New Jersey, Station WOR, March 24, 1941, 2. WPT archives.

148. The flower that White calls Tiger Lily is presently known as Turk's-cap Lily.

149. Elizabeth C. White, "Some Bog Plants of the Jersey Pines," *Wise-Acres*, publication of the Pennsylvania School of Horticulture for Women (Ambler, PA, 1929): 70. White used Witmer Stone's botanical plant names in *Plants of Southern New Jersey* (1911); where needed, these have been updated to modern taxonomic identifications as well as common names in accordance with Alan Weakley's *Flora*

of the Southern and Mid-Atlantic States (2015).

150. Dwarf Laurel is today known as Sheep Laurel (*Kalmia angustifolia*).

151. The Huckleberry that White refers to, *Gaylussacia baccata*, is the Black Huckleberry.

152. White, "Some Bog Plants of the Jersey Pines," 71.

153. Swamp Cedars are today known as Atlantic White Cedar (*Chamaecyparis thyoides*).

154. The bushes were 'Haines #9,' an early variety of blueberry cultivated by White and Coville.

155. White, "My Garden of Pine Barren Plants," 1.

156. Ibid., 2.

157. Ibid., 2–3.

158. Ibid., 3.

159. Robert Frost, *A Boy's Will* (New York: Henry Holt and Company, 1915), 25–26.

160. White, "My Garden of Pine Barrens Plants," 3–4.

161. Ibid., 4–5.

162. Elizabeth preferred the spelling Pixie, rather than the more common Pyxie.

163. Elizabeth C. White, "Plants of the New Jersey Pine Barrens," *Bulletin of the American Rock Garden Society*, 1, no. 2 (May–June 1943), 54.

164. White, "My Garden of Pine Barrens Plants," 2. This bog, affectionately known as "Old Bog," is no longer being cultivated, but the same panorama can be seen from the windows of the upper floors of Suningive, replacing Fenwick's bog with those in actual production today. They just aren't close enough to be considered Suningive's lawn.

165. This is the Threadleaf Sundew. Elizabeth Kite, "Sights and Sounds of Bogland," 2. WPT archives.

166. Letter from Elizabeth C. White to Chester M. Chaney, September 13, 1932, WPT archives.

167. Elizabeth C. White, "Taming Blueberries," transcript

of program of the Garden Club of New Jersey broadcast over WOR, Newark, NJ, July 6, 1937.

168. Charles P. Shoffner was farm and gardening editor for WCAU from 1923 until his death in 1946. He was known as the "dean of farm broadcasts."

169. Radio Broadcast, October 10, 1941 over WCAU (Philadelphia) by Miss Elizabeth C. White, Whitesbog, N.J. WPT archives.

170. Despite the longevity of their friendship, White and Wheeler remained formal in their correspondence. It was always Miss White and Mr. Wheeler.

171. Wheeler-ECW letters WPT archives: 1984.3.1.

172. Sash house. Structure used to protect plants from the weather and to get them adjusted to the environment before planting outdoors.

173. Letter from Elizabeth C. White to Wilfred Wheeler, January 21, 1939. WPT archives: 1984.3.23.

174. Various Letters between Wheeler and White. WPT archives: 1984.3.

175. Letter from Elizabeth White to Wilfrid Wheeler dated November 21, 1941. WPT archives: 1984.3.38.

176. The name was specifically chosen with "of America," rather than the American Holly Society so that the focus of the organization was not seen as limited to the study and propagation of *Ilex opaca*, native American holly.

177. Charles Young was a forester for the city of Baltimore.

Penn Trees

178. Edward Embree Wildman, *Penn's Woods 1682–1932* (Philadelphia: Christopher Sower Company, 1933), 89.

179. Letter, May 2, 1940. WPT archives: 1984.3.79.

Elizabeth C. White: A Life Well Lived

180. Notice in each issue read: "Pictures sent for criticism—

not more than two at one time—. . . unless otherwise advised, we shall consider ourselves at liberty to reproduce them in The American Amateur Photographer."

181. *The American Amateur Photographer*, vol. X, no. 12 (December 1898), The Outing Company Limited, New York, NY, 573.

182. *The American Amateur Photographer*, vol. XI, no. 1 (January 1899), The Outing Company Limited Company, New York, NY, 29.

183. We can't always tell a pet's gender from its name; this is true of the White's pet. Listed photos 90, 91, and 92 taken in March 1897, which we do not have, are of Don's puppies.

184. Rebecca was the daughter of J. J.'s brother, George; Mary and Howard were children of his eldest brother, Howard. There were no close relatives on her Mother's side of the family since the Fenwick's only other child, Thane, had died as a young man and never married. Later in life, Miss White would trace her maternal ancestry and would develop relationships with that part of the family.

185. The façade of the Marlborough-Blenheim inspired the "Ritz-Carlton" in the HBO show *Boardwalk Empire*.

Epilogue

186. Letter to Mr. Guy Nash, Wisconsin Cranberry Growers, December 29, 1923. WPT archives: 1984.2.13.

187. Elizabeth C. White, *Cranberries and Colony Contributions*, 4.

In Memoriam Albertine Senske

As the archivist for the Whitesbog Preservation Trust, Albertine Senske was in the perfect place to learn, consider, and eventually write about the life of Elizabeth Coleman White. Albertine worked tirelessly to identify, understand, and order innumerable details that told the story of Whitesbog. John Joyce has described her volunteer work, "cobbling together" information collected over the years. "Albertine," he writes, "almost single-handedly developed and organized the Whitesbog archives into an organized historical record that will benefit the Trust and future researchers for decades to come." Her dedication to this historical project was unsurpassed. As Ted Gordon, noted local historian, has stated, her willingness to assist researchers was unfailing.

Albertine was a talented and passionate speaker when introducing audiences to the history of Whitesbog and especially to Elizabeth White. Mark Ehlenfeldt describes her speaking style:

She usually started her talks much as anyone would, but before long, it was clear that she wasn't just lecturing, *she was testifying*. She would be leaning forward, gesturing, poking at the air, and robustly raising her voice for emphasis. She was fired up, and she clearly made the story of Elizabeth White come vibrantly to life for the people that came to hear her.

Albertine Senske was born, raised, and educated in Philadelphia. Her career path brought her into classrooms, teaching elementary and high school students in Pennsylvania and New Jersey. After retiring from the classroom, Albertine continued her own education, becoming a computer programmer for Prudential Insurance Company in Newark, New Jersey. Albertine never tired of learning. Further into her "retirement," she became a medical claims processor, bringing her to the office of a breast surgeon where, with her delicate and sensitive ways, she was always available for the patients who were experiencing a frightening illness. When medical insurance was a problem, she pursued every avenue to help patients.

Albertine was a deeply religious woman. With her never-ending desire to keep learning, she enrolled at Seton Hall University and took courses in Scripture, achieving her goal of becoming a Scripture Scholar. When she moved to her home in Whiting, New Jersey, Albertine began to work in the Helping Hands ministry of her parish, where, several days a week, she would shop for the homebound, take them to doctors' appointments, or just spend time sitting and listening to their stories.

In 2000, she discovered Whitesbog. Albertine began to volunteer there, working in the country store, giving tours, and teaching children about the blueberry and cranberry bogs. She became fascinated with the life and adventures of Elizabeth White, and began the research that suffuses this book, *With Eager Hands: The Life of Elizabeth Coleman White.* Her last years at Whitesbog were spent working in the archives in order to pre-serve the history of Whitesbog for future generations. As a tribute after her death, the Whitesbog Board of Trustees dedicated the archive facility at Suningive as the *"Albertine Senske Memorial Archive Room."* Sharon Goodman attests that "Being the archivist at Whitesbog may have been Albertine's last 'job,' but it was just as important to her as any of her other 'jobs.' "

Writing in the *Whitesbog Preservation Trust News-letter,* alongside other tributes quoted here, Terri Chiddenton presents an inventive, but fitting view of Albertine:

> In my mind's eye, I see this brilliant woman, this faithful servant of God, holding an in-depth, but pleasant conversation with another brilliant lady. I can hear Albertine questioning Elizabeth on all the uncertainties she must have formulated throughout her years of research, requesting the answers that she was never sure she had correct. And I smile when I think of Elizabeth gently taking Albertine's hand, and replying, "My dear, you probably comprehend my family with greater clarity than I ever did! You have made the White family members the esteemed legends they are today.

Albertine was a person who never shied away from challenges, including those she faced with her own disability. Everyone who knew her saw a faith-filled woman, a selfless giving person, a woman of determination and courage, a woman to imitate. Hers was a life well spent.

Madeline Fuccile and Lucille Covillo wrote the preponderance of this remembrance of their long-time friend, Albertine Senske. Additional information from Terry Chiddenton, Mark Ehelenfeldt, Janet Felt, Sharon Goodman, Ted Gordon and John Joyce was found in the Whitesbog Preservation Trust Newsletter, *second quarter, 2018.*

Afterword

Kiyomi Locker,
Archivist, Whitesbog Preservation Trust

Having read about the passion and mission of Elizabeth White, I hope you are inspired. In my time as Whitebog's resident Archivist and Historian (brief when compared with Albertine Senske's tenure), I have been continuously inspired by Elizabeth's story and her ingenuity in a field dominated by men. Ahead of her time, Elizabeth C. White was a woman whom history books should praise, yet she has been somewhat forgotten to the world, set aside in the annals of history. At a time when the reputations of many historic figures are being reexamined, and not always favorably, Elizabeth Coleman White is a woman about whom not one bad thing has been said. She was compassionate, but firm. She was intelligent and driven. She was a force to be reckoned with and a fitting role model for young women and men alike. All of those who pass through Whitesbog find Elizabeth's story inspiring and her lack of recognition disappointing.

The Archives of the Whitesbog Preservation Trust are filled not only with materials that tell Elizabeth's story, but also stories of the Pine Barrens and New Jersey as a whole. The accounts of those who lived and worked at Whitesbog, from 1857 to the present day, continue to enchant visitors. My goal as Archivist is to collect and share these stories, always centering on our main goal: preserving the legacy of Whitesbog.

I never had the opportunity to meet Albertine Senske, but wish I had. I only came on board at Whitesbog because she left a gaping hole in the organization. Her passion was unparalleled and most evident, I think, in the pages of this book. With its publication, the goal at the end of her life is complete. She left the book not quite finished, which allowed me and other members of the Whitesbog team to contribute the final details. I would like to thank Sarah Augustine, Sharon Goodman, and Janet Felt for all of their hard work and many days spent pouring over the Whitesbog collection. I know Albertine appreciates our efforts and I am proud to have been able to work with these colleagues to finish her project.

Colophon

Olivia Oravets completed initial line editing; Paul W. Schopp and Brendan Honick undertook additional editing. Proofreading was completed by Louis Burgess, Nicholas Caputo, Amanda Clark, Sarahjane Hehre, Michael Lorge, Emily Luberto, Emily Montgomery and Jessica Chamberlain. Kiyomi Locker, Sharon Goodman, Janet Felt, Sarah Augustine, Mark Ehlenfeldt and Allison Pierson helped to verify details using the Whitesbog Preservation Trust archives. Tom Kinsella designed, laid out the text, and supervised publication.

The text is set in 12-, 11-, and 10-point Adobe Garamond Pro. Cover design by Heidi Hartley.

Our Mission

The mission of the South Jersey Culture & History Center is to help foster awareness within local communities of the rich cultural and historical heritage of southern New Jersey, to promote the study of this heritage, especially among area students, and to produce publishable materials that provide a lasting and deepened understanding of this heritage.

CPSIA information can be obtained
at www.ICGtesting.com
Printed in the USA
LVHW030335011221
704845LV00001B/5